Dec 86

THE CHILDREN'S PICTURE BOOK

HOW TO WRITE IT, HOW TO SELL IT

by Ellen E.M. Roberts

Writer's Digest Books

Cincinnati, Ohio

Book design by Hal Siegel

First printing, October, 1981
Second printing, April, 1982
Third printing, April, 1984
First paperback printing, October, 1986

Library of Congress Cataloging in Publication Data

Roberts, Ellen E.M., 1946-
    The children's picture book.

    Bibliography: p.
    Includes index.
    1. Picture-books for children—Authorship.
I. Title.
PN147.5.R6   1981   808.06'8   81-11648
ISBN 0-89879-254-1   AACR2

ACKNOWLEDGMENTS

This book grew out of my twelve years as an editor and publisher of children's picture books. Rather than list here the many people who have influenced me, I have tried to include them in the pages that follow.

I was fortunate in having two excellent editors working on this book with me: Howard I. Wells III of Writer's Digest Books, who oversaw the long process of putting its many pieces together, and Anne Lunt. Twelve years ago, with her vast experience at Knopf, Viking, and Scribners, Anne Lunt introduced me to the world of children's books at St. Martin's Press. I am pleased that we had a chance to collaborate, in the true sense of the word, on this fascinating project.

Parts of this book have developed from lectures and workshops I have given over the last decade. I would like to thank Philip Sadler of Central Missouri State University for the opportunity to deliver the speech from which Chapter 10 grew; I would like to thank the Associated Children's Book Writers of Houston for the opportunity to try out the ideas which now appear in Chapters 9 and 11; and I would especially like to thank Jim and Faye Venable for their hospitality in Houston.

The Children's Book Guild in Washington, D.C., listened patiently to the beginning outlines of this book, and there Peggy and John Thomson were my peerless hosts.

Dale Payson and her class in children's book illustration at the School of Visual Arts in New York City; and Dr. Barbara Grant's graduate classes at William Paterson College who were my guinea pigs for Chapter 14; their interest and enthusiasm were invaluable.

I would also like to thank Janet Chenery and Claudia Lewis for reading and commenting on an early draft of this book.

The many writers and illustrators who discussed their work for this volume are mentioned in the text; I would like to spend a little space to mention those people whose names you won't see in print: Margaret Siewert, whose aid in incorporating early childhood education information was unstinting; Beatrice Hurford, whose enthusiasm for the project kept me going; Bill Hooks and Betty Boeghold of the Bank Street College of Education, who gave me an opportunity to see writers at work; and my family, whose bad jokes and good advice made all the difference.

A Note on the Illustrations:
Children's books have exerted their powerful spell on a wide range of artists and illustrators over the years. The uncaptioned illustrations throughout the book have been included to give the reader a taste of that range and diversity. They may also serve as a reminder of the inescapable interplay of words and pictures in this field.

for Paul

CONTENTS

Foreword by Barbara Rollock
Preface by Alvin Tresselt

PART ONE: GETTING THE PICTURE

PART TWO: PICTURE PERFECT, LETTER PERFECT

why no professional *ever* submits original artwork to publishers). Multiple submissions: pro and con; the power of positive thinking; revising on speculation: is it worth it?

FOREWORD

" . . . and where is the use of a book, thought Alice, without pictures or conversations?" Lewis Carroll's nineteenth-century child may well have been echoing the sentiments of children entering the twenty-first century. What could be more meaningful to the child of the electronic age than visual images?

In the minds of many, the genre "picture book" is synonymous with an art form, which indeed it is. But its unique quality lies in that proper balance of text and pictures which Ellen Roberts discusses in this book, though her emphasis is on the words—the "conversations," as it were. Maurice Sendak is one outstanding example of a contemporary picture book creator who concurs with her about the importance of the words. He has described his own difficulty in finding the right words, as well as the time-consuming process of accomplishing that economy of words and precision of expression which sustains the rhythm or mood of the action effectively.

Whether the validity of a story lies in the words or the pictures is a perpetual topic for discussion among librarians. No Caldecott Award committee begins deliberations without first attempting to define the term "picture book": it has become as popular a conundrum as the proverbial chicken and egg.

Historically, picture books were viewed as the province of the prereading child, whose visual literacy surpassed his verbal skills. Alphabet and counting books of all kinds and simple books of nursery rhymes dominated a field whose specific purpose was the instruction of small children who are just beginning to read, to take on the difficult business of decoding words in a book.

Librarians, though opposed to didacticism in any form, nevertheless saw another value in picture books for children: the illustrations were considered a primary source for a child's introduction to art. Randolph Caldecott, Leslie Brooke, Walter Crane were among the 19th century artists who brought an added dimension of fine artwork to books for children. The continuing recognition of the illustrator's essential role in picture books is exemplified by the annual awarding in this country of the Randolph Caldecott Medal for the artist, or, in the British Commonwealth, by the presentation of the Kate Greenaway Medal for distinguished work in the illustration of children's books.

Prestigious awards such as these encourage librarians to buy what has been judged to be the best, and stimulate parent requests for all books so singularly cited. In some of these award books, the illustrations clearly are the dominant feature. For example, in Ezra Jack Keats's *The Snowy Day,* the images of angels Peter makes in the snow linger in the memory, though the words might not be remembered. Peter Spier's text for *Noah's Ark,* based on an ancient Dutch poem, is beautiful but remains obscure unless one is using the book. Long after the covers are closed, however, one remembers the humorous visual details of a busy, housekeeping Noah. And who could fail to remember the pleasant heftiness of James Marshall's *George and Martha* creations, even if they lacked the benefit of his brief and humorous text? Yet the initial impact of the picture book is a twofold one: for the young child, sharing such a book with an adult, there is the aural response to the words, as well as the visual involvement with the art.

As the quantity of children's books of all kinds multiplied, the numbers of picture books increased proportionately. The newer picture books attempted current themes reflecting the climate of the times in which they were being produced. The traditional ABC books, nursery rhymes, or cautionary tales either took on a new guise or gave way to books depicting different images of children and childhood. Doubtless, explorations in developmental psychology and cognitive learning influenced many of these books for the young. There were now books on feelings, sibling rivalry, and the problems of coping with childhood fears. Trick or toy books and books of nonsense also remained for the sheer enjoyment of children, as did some contemporary classics, like *Madeline* or *Curious George.* All have made book selection more varied and challenging. While the true picture book—one with simple text and illustrations—is still available for the very young child, the category now ranges from the wordless or one-word-on-a-page book for the smallest toddler, to the more sophisticated and intricate designs of a book such as Kit Williams's *Masquerade* for the older child or adult.

By and large, picture book shelves in libraries reflect the variety of artistic skills and themes in books published for children today. Librarians, however, while aware of the need to maintain the highest standards in selection of books for the young child just discovering books, also yield to practical pressures such as child appeal, public demand, and parental interests. A good picture-book section might well house some traditional publications or even early editions of Randolph Caldecott picture books, along with contemporary favorites like Gág's *Millions of Cats,* or Lobel's *Frog and Toad* books, or Carle's *Very Hungry Caterpillar.* Some cautious selection is required, too, from the growing numbers of books which may best be categorized as bibliotherapy.

Books in which children are depicted in changing family patterns or life-styles, involving working mothers, divorce, adoption, or even tightened purse strings (*Tight Times,* by Barbara Shook Hazen), are more and more available.

Literary or artistic quality aside, many of these books have to be judged by other criteria. Are they realistic rather than maudlin or simplistic? Are they within the realm of a small child's understanding? Unlike factual books on trucks or trains, which may be examined for authenticity along different lines, the librarian must bring a certain sensitivity to the issues being presented. Of course, childlike humor and nonsense must be represented in any picture-book collection as well as fantasy, which some authors have mastered.

Regardless of the scope and variety in theme and artwork, however, the true art of the picture book lies not merely in the design, style, technique, or interpretation, but in the language, which may be savored on the tongue by repetition or sounding—and recalled, for pondering or imagining—even as the pictures are reexplored and resourced.

I'm glad Ellen Roberts mentioned Beatrix Potter, perhaps the foremost exponent of word *and* picture painting. Consider Peter's predicament in *The Tale of Peter Rabbit,* which describes a chastened rabbit, contrasted to his good bunny siblings:

> I am sorry to say that Peter was not very well during the evening.
>
> His mother put him to bed, and made some camomile tea; and she gave a dose of it to Peter!
>
> "One table-spoonful to be taken at bedtime."
>
> But Flopsy, Mopsy, and Cotton-Tail had bread and milk and blackberries for supper.

The words could stand alone; the illustrations bring home the message.

—Barbara Rollock, Coordinator,
Children's Services, New York Public Library

PREFACE

Having written, edited, and taught, as well as lectured extensively about picture books, I'm confronted with the difficulty of presenting an excellent book on an ephemeral, though intriguing, subject—the children's picture book.

Anyone who has ever tried to write a picture book knows that it is not easy to write a successful one. For some—even experienced writers—it's impossible. It is harder yet to write *about* how to write a picture book. However, Ellen Roberts has managed to handle this elusive subject meaningfully, clearly, and concisely, bringing together as much wisdom on the subject as has ever been assembled in a single volume. Not only is there plenty for the new writer in the pages that follow, but even the seasoned writer who has never quite been able to get a picture book text off the ground can learn much from Ellen Roberts.

Any book, of course, is a personal statement—a view of the situation as seen by the author—and this book is no exception. I might have stated such-and-such a bit differently, I might have emphasized this over that, I might have cited different examples, but nonetheless, I find myself in agreement with much of what she has to say.

No one can really tell anyone else how to write a picture book, any more than one can tell another how to create a poem, but there is a good deal that can be learned about picture book writing, such as an understanding of what is appropriate, how it's done by others, and the uses (they aren't just for bedtime stories) of picture books. So, too, an understanding of the professional milieu and the publishing field can help the neophyte desirous of entering the special world of the picture book. For those writers who have misconceptions about how to create something meaningful in a thousand words or less, Ellen has endeavored to set up guidelines to put them on the right track.

While the latter part of the book deals largely with the after-the-fact phase—what goes on after that heady letter of acceptance has arrived—it should be read carefully for the insight it gives into what goes on in an editorial office besides the reading of manuscripts. With some appreciation of these activities, you can, perhaps, approach an editor with less apprehension. Editors are very real people, and while they are never willfully short and unpleasant, they have pressures and demands on their time, so on occasion you might have the feeling you're being brushed aside. By respecting the reality of the editor's position and talents, you will find it easier to establish a relationship beneficial to both of you.

In my years as a writer of picture books, as an editor working with picture books written by others, and now as a teacher of aspiring writers, many of whom wish to write picture books, I have never found an ideal text on the subject, so this book will at last take care of a long-neglected area.

Not only aspiring picture book writers will gain from Ellen Roberts's yeoman job. During my years as editor at Parents' Magazine Press, countless picture book manuscripts flooded the office. While I found a few nuggets in the slush pile, which I accepted and published, the overwhelming majority of manuscripts were so far off base I sometimes got the impression that there were people out there trying to write picture book stories who had never so much as opened a picture book to see what was inside. If this book helps to raise the quality of submitted manuscripts, children's-book editors across the country will give a lusty cheer, I'm sure.

A book that deals with writing is a how-to book, but there is one big and important difference. You can read about how to set up a terrarium, how to construct a harpsichord, or how to build a doghouse, and the chances are that by following the instructions step by step you will end up with a flourishing terrarium, a harpsichord capable of playing Bach and Telemann, and a doghouse that suits Fido to a T. A book telling how to go about writing picture books carries no such assurances.

People's backgrounds, work habits, experience of books and children, and so on vary greatly, and no one can state categorically or exactly how to go about producing a manuscript for a picture book—especially a picture book, I think, because its demands are so special, its form so restrictive. It requires content that is within the grasp and interest of the two- to eight-year-old. It must be simple but never simplistic. Unlike most other books for children, the picture book is almost invariably read aloud, and this is partly why the text must be as multileveled as poetry. The content, style, and language must hold a child's interest, even through repeated readings, and the book must offer the adult who is doing the reading something, too—and that is where the writer's artistry is put to the test. Obviously such intangibles can't be taught the way a mathematical algorithm can, but Ellen Roberts has set down guidelines and suggestions for the writer which, while explicit, are at the same time flexible enough for the individual writer to adapt to his particular situation.

Reading this book will not guarantee that you can sit down at your typewriter and in short order come up with a masterpiece to set the picture book crowd on its ear, but it will certainly point you in the direction of success. By paying close attention to what Ellen has to say about working with this fragile and constraining form, you stand a good chance of producing a manuscript that pleases not only you and the editor who accepts it, but—most importantly—the child who will ultimately enjoy it.

—Alvin Tresselt, Dean of Faculty,
Institute of Children's Literature

PART ONE

GETTING THE PICTURE

Introduction:
What Is a Picture Book?

He hung about the library: handled the books; deranged the papers; ransacked the drawers; searched the old purses and pocketbooks for foreign coins; drew the sword-cane; snapped the traveling pistols; upset everything in the corners, and penetrated the President's dressing closet where a row of tumblers, inverted on the shelf, covered caterpillars which were supposed to become moths or butterflies, but never did.

Thus Henry Adams, a century and a half ago, began his lifelong friendship with books. "The intense blue of the sea," he writes in *The Education of Henry Adams,* "a mile or two away from the Quincy hills; the cumuli in a June afternoon sky; the strong reds and greens and purples of the children's picture books, as American colors then ran: these were ideals." Today these ideals have competition that is different from, but as compelling as, the foreign coins and caterpillars that distracted young Adams: television, comic books, baseball games, and Space Invaders all lure children away from books. But the ideals remain. The sharp and enduring images of an early book spur further reading, wider vistas. The experience becomes a series of experiences, a body of knowledge, a way of life. Reading gives information, from how to can pawpaws to how to measure the surface of a soap bubble. And reading gives pleasure, from mindless escape into fantasy to in-depth exploration of a new idea. Reading is substantial, enduring, and various. It's a habit parents want their children to acquire, not just because it is good for them, but because it is good, period. The picture book was developed, in part, to help children learn to read, and was refined to make them *want* to read. And it was developed to give them pleasure.

By the time the quality picture book became established in the United States, it was already an evolved form. It was either small like Greenaway's *A = Apple Pie,* for children to hold in their little hands or large, like Boutet de Monvel's *Aesop's Fables,* so that immature eyes

could easily see the print and examine the pictures. It was carefully delineated and often colored to catch attention. It was paced with great
care to hold attention. Sometimes it was so gentle it was boring, sometimes it was so violent it was frightening. But its aim, whichever extreme
or in between, was to reflect the interests of childhood from an adult's
point of view.

You are lucky to be writing for young children, because they are
the one segment of our population that is actively encouraged to read.
Parents, eager for their children to do well in school, introduce them to
the reading habit early through picture books. Teachers, who see the
universal childhood enthusiasm for a story in class after class, year after
year, allow time in their curriculums for reading for fun and storytelling
units; librarians pitch books to young children with admirable zeal; and
older brothers and sisters who know the magic of reading firsthand are
usually eager to initiate the preschooler into the circle of readers. Compare the way an adult approaches a children's picture book and the
way a child does. You will see how much stronger the appeal of pictures
is to children than it is to the adult.

How Adults Read Picture Books

Have you ever asked an adult friend to read a picture book? I
have. "What's this?" a grown-up reader asks, picking up a copy of
Blueberries for Sal, by Robert McCloskey, from my coffee table.

"That's a great book!" I say. "You should read it." Still standing, he thumbs through the book.

"It's cute," he admits, and sets the book down, without having
read a single word. In my house, this is not allowed. "Read it," I command. Starting from the back, he obediently flips through the pages.

"Gee, it has hardly any words in it," he says. Will this get him off
the hook?

"It will take you two minutes to read," I reply between gritted
teeth. This is a challenge. No one can resist the chance to show off his
reading speed. I sit my friend down, place the book in his lap, and open
it to page 1. Trapped, he reads it. It doesn't take two minutes, it takes
ten, because he takes time to marvel at the way this small book says so
much.

"This is fantastic! Who's the guy who wrote this book? Where
can I get a copy for my daughter? How did he think of this? Wow, if I'd
read this when I was a kid, I'd be living in Maine now. Do you know
how long it's been since I've had fresh blueberries? This is a great
story!"

I shut up and smile.

I've seen the scene acted out hundreds of times, and I expect to see it thousands more. It raises the question picture book authors have to face: if the writing is so good, why does it have to have pictures? The simple answer is that children like pictures, they are comfortable with pictures, in a way many adults have forgotten. Is the picture book writer only writing captions for the illustrator's pictures, then? Is that old adage about a picture being worth a thousand words true?

Sure it is. Even in our adult lives, there are instances where we prefer pictures. Assured by a friend that her house is just seven easy turns off the main road, we listen bemusedly to a succession of "sharp rights" and "bear lefts," then ask her for a map. When we need to replace the thingamajig on the dishwasher, we take a rough drawing of it along to the store to make sure we get the right one. Pictures, blueprints, maps, diagrams, and operating instructions describing the single right way a thing must hang together are useful in situations where words, with their wonderful ambiguity, are inadequate. A picture leaves no room for error.

And there is more to it. As adults we turn to pictures for information it would take paragraphs, chapters, volumes to describe. A photograph of a friend tells us something that a letter can't. A television newsclip of a riot in a far-off land brings it to life. A child's drawing can give us insights that it would take hours of conversation to unearth. A picture can be exact, and a picture can be infinitely evocative. The wiring diagram for the stereo is exact; a portrait of Napoleon is evocative. Neither means as much to a child as it does to you, because experience has provided you with a set of analogies and insights a child hasn't collected yet. If you didn't understand the conventions of a wiring diagram, the stereo hookup could be disastrous; if you hadn't studied Napoleon's life in school, he'd be just another man with medals.

How Children Relate to Pictures

Initially a child reads a picture book because it has pictures in it. A picture is a lure, an instantaneous glimpse of a complex situation, a door that opens to the view beyond. The picture book uses illustrations to draw children into the world of words. For a child to whom reading is uncharted territory, the pictures provide a map of what's to come.

This is an important reassurance to the beginning reader, between the ages of two and eight. He is feeling uncertain about reading. He may encounter words he doesn't know. The title only hints at the content, and the only way he can estimate whether he will like the book is to check out the pictures. After he's decided from the pictures that he's interested in reading this particular book, they help him past troublesome patches by giving him clues about what is going on in the story. The visual identification with the characters, reinforced by their appearance page after page, motivates him to get through parts of the story that he finds difficult or slow. Picture book pictures help a child *want* to read, and then they help him *to* read. The pictures are at once exciting and reassuring, all in the cause of helping the child appreciate your story.

Writing appears in book form so that it can endure. It endures for the moment so that the child can concentrate on a particular page that holds his interest; it endures for months so that he can read and reread it until he knows your words by heart; it endures for years so that he can share it with a sister or a friend; and it endures for generations so that he can pass it on to his children and their children.

The illustrations in the children's picture book invite the child in; the words invite him to stay, and to come back again.

Who Writes Picture Books?

Such writers as Margaret Wise Brown, Dr. Seuss, Ruth Krauss, and Robert McCloskey have created worlds in children's books that have inspired generations of children to love reading and writing. How they've achieved this is summarized by Charlotte Zolotow, author of more than fifty books for children of the picture book age: "I write for the child in me."

Writing *by* children, as author Claudia Lewis carefully explains in *Writing for Young Children,* has a special life and insight that most adults lose as they pursue logic, experience, and good sense. There are some adults who haven't lost this special insight and never will. They are the ones who write *for* children. Usually they are people who do something else, too: they draw, they teach, they raise children, they write advertising copy or serious novels. They are lawyers, bus drivers, doctors, students. They are young, they are old, they are rich, they are poor, they live alone, they live with three brothers, six children, twenty pet chinchillas.

There are some ways in which picture book authors are very much alike, but no sociologist could profile the similarities. If a writer of adult nonfiction or a novelist for older children came into my office wearing a new pair of shoes, he'd most likely never mention it. But when a picture book author I know came into my office one day, he not only mentioned it, but went on to twirl and turn, made me guess how many pairs he'd tried on before he chose them, and then asked to see *my* shoes. Picture book authors are spontaneous, interested in the minutiae of life, and eager to share the simple pleasures and great joys of being alive. When the press of business overwhelms me and I want to go out to lunch just for fun, I always call up a picture book author. And, resourceful people that they are, they are usually able to juggle their schedules for a spur-of-the-moment editorial lunch, to discuss the myriad new ideas that every picture book author has.

Behind the spontaneous exterior, though, the typical picture book author is serious-minded. Picture book authors are people who remember. We were all three years old once, then seven, then thirteen, but most of us are so preoccupied with adult matters—from having the tires rotated, to planning the dinner menu, to understanding the energy crisis—that the memory is overwhelmed. Not the picture book author: he can tell you how the sun slanted the first time he climbed to the top of the jungle gym, or how his grandmother's hand felt when he crossed the street with her thirty-five years ago. He may be known to lose his glasses or lock the keys in the car, but no detail escapes him.

The picture book author's seriousness is no secret from editors. The talent it takes to write for young children in the first place, and the professionalism and confidence that are then required to make the manuscript exactly right, are rare. When an editor "discovers" a picture book author, he values him highly. The long and close associations between children's book editors and their authors withstand trends, fads, and changing approaches to marketing books and educating children.

Today's picture book author is venturing into a field that is increasingly competitive, surprising, and expanding. Once a quiet corner of publishing, dominated by a small band of dedicated editors, artists, writers, and librarians, children's picture book publishing has become a major area for many publishers, with new markets springing up everywhere. The librarian, once the primary arbiter of what *should* be published (basing his opinion on what children *should* be reading), is now just one of the many customers publishers seek to please. Now the editor listens not only to librarians who want to keep their book collections circulating, but also to teachers who want to inspire young children to read for pleasure as well as for information, parents who want their children to get the book habit early, and children themselves who want to read about the multitudinous and surprisingly sophisticated subjects that capture their interest. Including—and we'll get back to this later—subjects that have captured their interest via that supposed enemy of literature, television.

The needs of young children are constant from generation to generation; the traditional standards continue to apply. *Peter Rabbit* is still going strong after three-quarters of a century. But society is constantly changing, and the author must also write to fit the special needs of today's children. *In The Night Kitchen* and *The Stupids Step Out,* two contemporary classics, are appealing to a new generation of children at the same time as *Millions of Cats* and *And To Think That I Saw It on Mulberry Street,* which were written fifty years ago.

These days, picture book editors are less likely to assign topics than they are to seek out the unique concept, the unusual slant. Editors are counting on authors more and more for regional subjects, colorful characters, and original approaches to spice up their lists. But they are frustrated by the inappropriateness of most manuscripts submitted for publication as picture books. The writer who understands which conventions are inviolable and which rules can be stretched to accommodate a new idea is at a tremendous advantage.

What to Expect from the Illustrator

The notion that a dismal text can make a plausible picture book if it is well illustrated is a misconception. It is widely held among publishers, editors, illustrators, and—saddest of all—writers. Librarians know better, and every respected reviewer of children's books judges the text first. Sure, a sloppy story about Johnny's new tooth can have stunning illustrations, but if the book doesn't pass the "text test," the pictures will never reach the audience they deserve.

Experienced illustrators know that if the story isn't simply wonderful, the book doesn't have a chance. An illustrator will spend days, months, sometimes even years creating pictures for your words, so he's going to consider those words very carefully before he commits his time to them. There are hacks and desperate newcomers in the illustration field just as there are in any other, but the professional standards that have evolved under the fierce guardianship of parents, librarians, teachers, and reviewers remind the illustrator that his survival depends on being a tough critic of your writing. If it doesn't measure up to the standards he has set for himself, he won't have a thing to do with it.

What can you do to ensure that your story has the most appropriate and attractive illustrations possible? It starts with your relationship with your editor. Editors are inclined to keep authors and artists as far away from one another as possible. The reason for this is obvious: an editor doesn't want to be caught in the middle of a custody battle. The picture book writer has to have a strong visual sense in order to write for illustration, and the illustrator has to have a strong literary bent in order to prefer illustrating books to painting landscapes or drawing courtroom scenes. Too often, the opposing opinions that emerge from these overlapping interests in the other's art can be fighting words.

Many writers get their picture books off to a bad start by insisting that the art professor at the local college or the textbook illustrator from down the street is the only person to illustrate their story. Some writers go in the opposite direction and demand that the editor assign a famous illustrator to their book to ensure good sales. Neither of these is a promising tack. Stay loose! Your editor wants to make the perfect match as much as you do, and will welcome your suggestions, since you know the manuscript better than anyone. "Wouldn't line illustrations help get these concepts over best?" you can ask. Or, "I've tried to keep the spirit of the manuscript as light as possible, so perhaps cartoon illustrations would be most effective." Don't make suggestions that beg for a negative answer, and stick with what you, the writer, feel is best for your manuscript. If you back up your case with good reasons and informed precedents, the editor will welcome your views. If you try to do the editor's—or worse still, the illustrator's—job for him, you are going to find your calls not returned, your letters unanswered.

Let me tell you how one author overcame what seemed to be an impossible obstacle. This author (who wants to remain anonymous) had told a very contemporary story about a middle-class family facing the father's layoff. One of her favorite illustrators was assigned to the book, and the author was ecstatic—until she saw the rough illustrations. The illustrator had missed the author's point, which the writer had made very quietly in order to keep her story from becoming a sociological tract. The illustrations showed a poverty-level family in an urban neighborhood. The author was upset, but you would never know it from the way she approached her editor: "There are so many books about poor families facing loss of income," she explained. "I worry that the book will be lost in the shuffle without my special angle." She didn't flaunt her artistic integrity; she didn't accuse the editor of being uncaring. The editor had a talk with the artist, and the book is a knockout. The writer had faith in her work, and the quiet might of a person who knows she's right. A temper tantrum, or laying down the law, would have achieved nothing but high blood pressure and a higher phone bill. She got mad first, and then summoned all the tact she could to state her case.

Between the Lines

Sometimes the author has gripes about the illustrations that are matters of fact, not matters of interpretation or taste. Nonny Hogrogian, an illustrator who's written books herself, tells how she and Sorche NicLeodhas, her collaborator, got off on the wrong foot at first. "I take great pride in doing careful research," Hogrogian recalls, "and when Miss NicLeodhas informed me that the bone structure of my first Scotsman was more like that of a Rumanian than a Scot, I was crushed. I promised myself I would never make a mistake like that again." Hogrogian and NicLeodhas didn't let this initial upset get in the way of future collaborations, and their second book, *Always Room for One More,* won the Caldecott Medal.

The precision of your images creates specific images in your reader's mind, and one of your first and most important readers is the illustrator. With carefully chosen words to work with, the illustrator can draw a character who lives and breathes, a landscape with weather, a puppy so lost that the reader aches to reach out and rescue him. The illustrator is your ally, building the bridge between the world your young reader has experienced—the world of seeing and feeling—and the world you have built for her to discover—the world of thinking and dreaming.

The Limitations—and the Possibilities—of the Picture Book

The most basic limitation for the picture book manuscript is length. The standard thirty-two-page picture book contains only about twenty-five pages of actual text. The space on these pages is divided about equally between words (in large type with generous spacing) and pictures. The number of words in a picture book manuscript, then, ranges from no words at all to a thousand. The commonest range is from about a hundred to four hundred words. A sentence or two per page, a paragraph per double-page spread: this is the rule of thumb. The picture book writer, then, must be a blend of short story writer and poet. His organization must be tight; he must be economical, and must give meaning to every word. He has to be sensitive to the nuances of language, its overtones and undertones, finding just the right word, the perfect image to conjure up the mental picture and inspire the artist to create the actual one. Verbosity is verboten! The picture book must be arresting, even spellbinding, in its progress from point to point, and it must be pleasing to the ear. The picture book is a book that is read aloud, over and over. It requires the rhythm and economy of a poem, even if it's straight prose.

A second constraint is the age group of the audience. The picture book writer is addressing children, first and last. But adults are reading the book, too. Parents and grandparents, aunts and uncles, teachers and librarians are the major purchasers of books, and during picture book age, children usually share the book with an adult at story hour, at bedtime, or in school. Within the conventionally limited vocabulary and the small number of words, the author has to please children without boring or alienating adults. The parent reading *The Story of Babar* for the fortieth time in a month appreciates Jean de Brunhoff's economy, originality, and style. The teacher who reads Marjorie Flack's *Story about Ping* to her kindergarten class every spring chooses this story over others not only because the children like it, but because *she* likes it. Like a poem or short story, it is both spare and rich. And the richness resides in its evocative power. But the limitations of space and vocabulary notwithstanding, the picture book writer faces an almost alarming *lack* of limitations. This season's diverse crop of picture books includes a beautifully illustrated volume on blowing up buildings, a Chinese folktale about a painter with a magic brush, and a retelling of an old family anecdote. A tractor, a princess, an alligator—the choice is yours. This book was written to help you make that choice, and to show you how to develop your manuscript once you've chosen what you want to write about. It contains no magic formulas, but it attempts to cover the subjects the writer—whether published or unpublished—may wonder about.

Senses 6 and 7

Is your smashing book idea really terrific, or is it a dud? Developing a sure sense of book ideas is lifeblood to the picture book author. That book sense is a dual one, because it's just as vital to know what ideas are good illustration potential as it is to understand which ones will click with children. What made Janice May Udry realize how superbly her simple idea of children dancing under a summer moon would lend itself to Sendak's lush, joyful illustration? What instinct told her that the concept would have so elemental and enduring an appeal? Her sixth/seventh sense led her to write *The Moon Jumpers.*

"What's your next book about?" an eager fan in a library convention audience demanded of Jan Wahl. Wahl, the author of a string of picture books including *Pleasant Fieldmouse* and *Jeremiah Knucklebones,* wasn't working on anything in particular just then, and for a moment he drew a blank. Then Senses 6 and 7 came to his rescue. *"Frankenstein's Dog* and *Dracula's Cat,"* he replied without missing a beat; and went home and wrote them. This on-the-spot inspiration led to a series that sells beautifully both here and abroad—thanks to Wahl's finely tuned picture book sense.

Understanding what lies between the lines in good picture book writing is second nature to professional picture book writers. Tomie de Paola, driving home during rush hour one evening ten years ago, imagined the littlest kid on the street with a wagonload of big alphabet blocks, an A, an N, a D, and a Y. The big kids take over his letters and add their own, spelling "handy," "candy," and other words—but they won't let him play, so he takes his blocks and goes home. De Paola wrote *Andy: That's My Name* between Boston and Cambridge, without ever taking his hands off the steering wheel. The actual execution took longer, of course, as he worked to make each spread logical and exciting, but his understanding of the principles of story and pictures brought him the concept in a sudden stroke of genius. "A sudden stroke of genius"; "a flash of inspiration"; "a writer's instinct"—clearly all these terms apply. Udry's instincts *were* sound, Wahl *was* inspired, de Paola *is* a genius; but don't make the mistake of writing it all off to some kind of writers' black magic. Hours and years of hard work and hard thought lay behind those three inspirations, and behind thousands of others. That sixth/seventh sense can and must be developed, because you can't write a decent line without it.

And how do you go about developing book sense? You read, read, read! You pore over every book mentioned in these pages (they're listed in the bibliography), and go to your library for more. You read, and analyze, and think, and read some more, and bit by bit, you will find your knowledge deepening, your book sense becoming surer.

And what a good time you'll have doing it!

What Can I Tell You?

I grew up in a reading family. No birthday or Christmas passed without the exchange of books. As important as books were in my childhood, they are an even more important part of my adult life. Almost every week a brand-new book arrives at my office at Prentice-Hall, smelling faintly of fresh glue and new paper, ready to be studied and savored, and compared and contrasted with the books I'm involved in producing. I write this book as an editor, an analyst and an advocate of good writing for children, not as a practitioner. I cannot tell you what it is like to have the talent and fire to write for children, or the discipline to stick with an idea until it is exactly right. But I *can* tell you about quality children's books—how they are written, how they are illustrated, and how they are published.

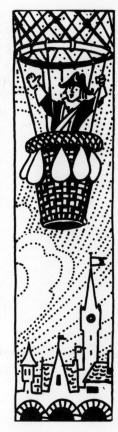

The book has two parts, two aims: The first is to explore the principles of good writing for young children and to acquaint you with what has been written for children up to now. No course of instruction, no system for writing can illuminate the principles of effective writing for the picture book age as well as a careful study of the existing first-rate picture books can. The annotated bibliography at the close of this volume will guide you to the titles I find especially appealing, and you will find others for yourself that you like even better. The final third of the book is a practical guide to publication. This section will help you through the maze of submission practices, contract conventions, and working in a team with an illustrator. This section is especially helpful to the writer who wants to make a career of writing for children. As ambitious as this may seem to a writer starting out in this field, you will find that one of the great satisfactions of writing for children is their loyalty to favorite authors. Rare is the writer who produces only one book for the picture book age. The world of the children's picture book is a fascinating one, and with this book at your elbow, you are ready to explore it for yourself.

1

The Whole Picture

The picture book audience is far from limited to little kids. When picture books get big and fat and as costly as dinner for two, they're called "coffee table books," but they are still picture books at heart—picture books for art lovers, for sports fans, for railroad enthusiasts, for history buffs. Coffee table books and quality children's books share some fundamental characteristics. They are large in format, with a picture on every two-page spread, and a text that is composed of, or includes, captions for the pictures. And picture books for children have some special qualities of their own.

The children's picture book is child-sized. Its format may be oversized—wider than six inches and taller than nine—but, in keeping with the child's attention span, it is never very long, with a maximum of sixty-four pages and a standard length of thirty-two pages. (As noted in Chapter 13, books are bound in signatures of eight pages, so anything from twenty-four to sixty-four pages, moving up by multiples of eight, can constitute a children's picture book.) The type in a children's picture book is large enough for the child who deciphers his words letter by letter and syllable by syllable to comprehend easily. To make each line of type distinct, picture book texts have wide spaces, or *leading* (pronounced "ledding"), between the lines.

These physical specifications—the small number of pages, the preponderance of illustrations, and the large size of the type—require the picture book writer to tell his story succinctly. A sentence up to a paragraph for each double-page spread: these word limitations in a picture book can't be overemphasized. Within these limitations, the writer must create a story that is substantial, moving, memorable. This is a tall order for a short book. Lisl Weil, the author of dozens of picture books, including *Things That Go Bang* and *Fat Ernest,* summarizes the most challenging aspect of writing for small children in a small space when she says, "I hope with my stories I give my readers and listeners something to think about."

To understand the full impact of this challenge, writers must re-member that their audience includes adults as well as children.

Has Television Killed Reading?

If you put a child in a room with twenty picture books and one television set, will he look at even one of the books? Even toys and games are often second-choice entertainments these days, but both toys and books gain a child's love in ways television never can. Chil-dren who sit in a parent's lap sharing a book have a very different expe-rience from the glassy-eyed family lined up in a row in front of the tele-vision, never conversing because the TV is too overpowering to inter-rupt.

Some writers condemn television out of hand because of its seeming monopoly on preschoolers' attention. This is nonsense. True, television has unseated books as the primary form of entertainment, but never forget that television can become tiresome. Love of books is so deep that it is an experience readers want to share, and it will take more than television to annihilate its appeal.

Far from supplanting books, television is excellent preparation for reading, as the success of "Sesame Street" shows. Whatever kind of show she is exposed to, the very young child quickly learns to "read" sequences of sophisticated graphics as well. Television is also a useful adjunct to reading. When Captain Kangaroo reads a story on his morn-ing television show, the child who has a quick glimpse of the pictures as they flit by on the screen is delighted to discover that he can hold that very same book in his own hands, and turn the pages at his own pace. In this way, books offer an alternative to one of television's frustrations, the immediate disappearance of images. A child can pore over the pic-tures in a book, study them, copy them, share them, and, best of all, return to them again and again. With a little encouragement, the child can go on to draw his own pictures, adapt the story for acting out, or write a story of his own. These secondary rewards of reading are deeply satisfying. Television offers a more powerful come-on than picture books, but once the book has been explored and enjoyed, it is a stal-wart friend. Television can never be more than a fickle companion.

Who Buys Children's Picture Books?

Children of the picture book age do not buy their own books. Though many parents encourage their children to select their own books at the library or bookstore, actual book purchases are made by parents and grandparents, uncles and aunts, neighbors and big brothers, and, most of all, teachers and librarians. Your book has to please children ultimately, but first it must win the approval of the adults and older children who actually purchase books for the very youngest reader. The fact that adults select books for the picture book age is one of the important reasons for the excellence of these books. An adult confronted with the possibility of reading a book many times is going to look for a book that promises *him* pleasure as well as the child. It is hard to imagine an adult reader getting bored with Ludwig Bemelmans's spirited account of Madeline's appendectomy in *Madeline,* or *The Tale of Benjamin Bunny* becoming a chore to read. The authors of these two books, working a generation apart, both knew the secret of writing for children: emphasizing directness and simplicity, without becoming repetitive or banal. "It is said that the eating of too much lettuce is soporific," Beatrix Potter informs us in *The Tale of the Flopsy Bunnies,* and reading this line for the hundredth time still brings a smile to an adult's face.

Librarians, by far the largest purchasers of picture books for children, are also critical customers. They make a careful study of children's literature in graduate school. They learn about reading levels, subject areas of interest to various age groups within the picture book range, problems encountered in getting children to start reading and the greater problem of getting them to *keep* reading. They apply high professional standards to book selection, and they monitor their collections carefully, always modifying their own judgments by the experiences their young patrons share with them. Librarians talk to children every day and never stop learning from them. Manning the circulation desk or supervising the children's room, the librarian is the first to know that the book that was a hit with four-year-olds three years ago is gathering dust today. The librarian notices that the promising picture book writer on whom he was keeping a careful eye is turning out less distinguished material, so he looks elsewhere for new talent. Toughest of critics, most faithful of fans, librarians keep on top of writing for the picture book age, ever on the lookout for books that combine high literary standards and child appeal.

Teachers love children's books just as librarians do, but their ultimate aim is slightly different from that of the children's specialist at the public library. The teacher and her ally, the school librarian, are concerned with the child's intellectual development, while the public librarian is primarily interested in fostering a child's leisure-time reading interests. Informational books, storybooks keyed to a child's reading level, and activity books that tie in with the early-childhood school curriculum are the picture books that are popular with teachers, whereas public librarians are looking for books that stretch the imagination and provide information a child needs to pursue his hobbies.

Parents, relatives, and friends of young children are the most expert buyers of all. They *know* the child for whom the book is intended, and want something that is just right. If Matthew is a seven-year-old hiking enthusiast, Taro Yashima's *Crow Boy,* with its marvelous description of a little boy who knows and loves the outdoors, is just the book for him. If Lucy is a romantic six-year-old who is old-fashioned enough to dream of a Prince Charming, Joe Lasker's *Merry Ever After,* the story of two medieval weddings full of pageantry and partying, will especially appeal to her. Three-year-old Benjamin, celebrating his birthday, will be captivated by Judi and Ron Barrett's *Benjamin's 365 Birthdays.* For parents, relatives, and friends, the criticism that there are too many books to choose from is nonsense: there's a just-right book for every child, geared to his interests and age level, executed to the adult purchaser's taste.

But the reality is that adult taste and child taste do not always coincide. "The children of the New York Public Library have made

Illustration 1-1.

In Higgelty Piggelty Pop!, *Maurice Sendak uses the conventions of comic book art by adding cartoon balloons to his elegant pen-and-ink drawings.*

Curious George the perennial favorite in our collection," Augusta Baker, the librarian there for many years, observes with a twinkle. Although this book has always been popular with youngsters, its appeal is lost on many adults. It is but one example of children having the last word in choosing the books they love.

Furthermore, a child who wouldn't be caught dead in the library may spend hours reading comic books, as picture book author Guy Billout did when he was a little boy. Billout's mother was the proprietor of a bookstore, and much to her chagrin, her son spent his spare time in the back of the store poring over comic books. Maurice Sendak was also a comic lover as a child; both of these writer-artists have made important contributions to children's picture books by drawing on their childhood passions. Sendak has introduced panels and balloons, conventions taken outright from comics, into his artwork in *Higglety Pigglety Pop!* (Illustration 1-1) and *In the Night Kitchen.* Billout has developed from another comic tradition the narrative flow of a story without words in his *Number 24,* the wordless story of a man who witnesses extraordinary events as he waits for a bus. Some comic books have been so successful that they have been issued as books for children: Tintin is popular with children in both comic and book form throughout the world. No question about it, children love the fast pace, colorful characterization, and surefire excitement of the comic book. They look for these same qualities in the picture book.

How Picture Books Developed

For the last century, the making of books for children has consistently attracted talented writers, designers, editors, and artists. A century ago in England, Walter Crane, Kate Greenaway, and Randolph Caldecott (for whom the coveted Caldecott Award is named) created the forerunners of the modern picture book for children. Traditional rhymes, illustrated fairy tales, and gloriously illustrated stories for older children dominated the field. In France, de Monvel illustrated carefully chosen tales from Aesop and history in almost animated sequences for children, in book form. In Germany, Heinrich Hoffmann created the colorful and cartoony *Strewwelpeter,* a collection of rather gory cautionary tales that still enjoys favor with children throughout the world.

By the turn of the century, Beatrix Potter and William Nicholson began to create storybooks for the very youngest readers that continue to be favorites today, *The Tale of Peter Rabbit* and *Clever Bill* epitomize what children like to hear and see, and what adults find delightful from the first reading on.

By the 1920s, American publishers had created special publish-

Peter Rabbit, the first of Beatrix Potter's twenty-plus stories for children, is distinguished by its gentle watercolors and naturalistic detail. The tiny format of these books by the English artist has become her trademark; often imitated, she has never been surpassed at blending realism and fantasy in a single illustration.

Maud and Miska Petersham create lovable animal friends for the baby in *The Box with Red Wheels*. When Mama closes the garden gate to keep the animals away from the baby, everyone is very sad. Reunited, Baby and animal friends are clearly enjoying each other's company.

The first DUCK nipped Angus's tail!

HISS-S-S-S-S-S!!!

HISS-S-S-S-S-S!

The second D
flappe

In *Angus and the Ducks,* Angus, "the very young little dog" created by Marjorie Flack, ventures beyond the hedge to encounter his first ducks in this simple and exciting picture book. Safely home, Angus crawls under the sofa and *For exactly THREE minutes by the clock, Angus was NOT curious about anything at all.* You can see why.

Lisa, the heroine of Don Freeman's *Corduroy,* chooses her very own bear from an endearing array of stuffed animals in this dramatic illustration at the close of the book. Soft colors and lively expressions are characteristic of Freeman's gentle touch in picture book illustration.

Feodor Rojankovsky uses color so skillfully that it's hard to isolate the cartoon conventions—like the whey spilling on Miss Muffet's shoes—which make his work so accessible to the very young. This exaggerated drawing in *The Tall Book of Mother Goose* has all the warmth of real life.

Holling Clancy Holling was the towering genius behind the nonfiction picture book, as this illustration from *Seabird* shows. Combining a story with information in the text, he also combines informational black-and-white drawings alongside dramatic full-color paintings to evoke the world of whaling.

Serene realism and compelling content mark the unforgettable illustrations for Maurice Sendak's *Outside Over There*. A rhythmic and compact text conveys a complex story through pictures that fill the page.

Thirty years after he originally illustrated *The Runaway Bunny* by Margaret Wise Brown, artist Clement Hurd reillustrated the story alternating black-and-white sketches on text pages with these cheerful full-color paintings of a little bunny's fantasies. The alternation gives the child a chance to exercise his imagination before the artist unfolds his.

William Steig utilizes the holding line characteristic of the cartoonist, but his inspired use of color elevates his illustration beyond the simple color-in cartoon. In *Sylvester and the Magic Pebble* he captures the mood of a spring picnic and the emotions of a family reunion with deceptive simplicity.

Taro Yashima is a wonderful storyteller who gives *Crow Boy*, a tale of a schoolboy outcast who wins acceptance, a special atmosphere with richly crayoned colors, telling details, and perspectives that share a childlike view of the world.

Virginia Lee Burton was a designer, writer, and illustrator noted
for her books that featured inanimate objects as leading characters.
In *The Little House* she brings a cottage to life as the countryside
surrounding it changes. Like many illustrators, she is concerned
with the integration of type and picture, and each double-page
spread is carefully planned as a unit.

Unconventional and unparalleled, Tomi Ungerer enjoys popularity with
children for his outrageous plots and detail-packed illustrations. In *The
Beast of Monsieur Racine,* he chronicles the adventures of a French
gentleman and his pet beast, here revealed to be two children in disguise. The highly controversial details in his illustrations keep children
looking for new nonsense on every page.

Old Julian, the gardener at the mission at Capistrano, and Juan, the hero of Leo Politi's *Song of the Swallows,* feed the birds. Dramatic perspective and loving detail in both composition and color distinguish this muted and memorable picture story.

Crunch, crunch, crunch, his feet sank into the snow.
He walked with his toes pointing out, like this:

He walked with his toes
pointing in, like that:

Silent snow and brightly colored clothes catch the eye in this illustration for *The Snowy Day* by Ezra Jack Keats. The contrast of the colors and the daring simplicity of the composition make this and other Keats illustrations especially appealing to the very young.

Naturalistic details and a cartoon caboose called Katy blend perfectly in this illustration by Bill Peet in *The Caboose Who Got Loose*. Peet draws the disparate elements together by giving the caboose a human character and capturing the animals in characteristic activities.

This graphic illustration from Donald Crews's *Freight Train* creates an authentic impression of cars in motion as they whiz by a cityscape. The reader feels the speed and smells the smoke through the innovative use of color and image.

Going by cities

ing departments to produce children's books. Anne Carroll Moore of the New York Public Library and Bertha Mahoney Miller in Boston issued lists of good reading fare for children, and writing for the youngest age came into its own as an American art. The pioneers in American picture book publishing were E. Boyd Smith, the author of *The Farm Book* and *Chicken World;* Kurt Wiese, who began his long career with *The Three Little Kittens,* Berta and Elmer Hader, who created *The Big Snow,* and Wanda Gág, whose *Millions of Cats* exemplifies economy and excellence as it sells through its fiftieth printing. The earliest creators of children's books were most often illustrators who could write as well; Marjorie Flack's *Story about Ping,* illustrated by Kurt Wiese, was the first collaboration of great success between a picture book writer and an artist. Munro Leaf, Margaret Wise Brown, and Alvin Tresselt perpetuated and developed this tradition of writing stories for children that someone else would illustrate, and their books, *The Story of Ferdinand, Goodnight Moon,* and *Rain Drop Splash,* show a writer's sensitivity to a child's taste in what he wants to read about, and how much can be said with a very few words.

By the 1950s, the children's picture book writer had become a precious commodity. Charlotte Zolotow's evocation of the ordinary in *One Step . . . Two,* Ruth Krauss's collection of children's definitions *A Hole Is to Dig,* and Marcia Brown's spirited retelling of fairy and folk tales brought high standards to the field, standards that were explored and expanded in the sixties by Ezra Jack Keats in *Pet Show,* by Maurice Sendak in *Where the Wild Things Are,* by Bernard Waber in *Lyle, Lyle, Crocodile,* by Bill Peet in *Merle, the High-Flying Squirrel,* and by Tomi Ungerer in *Moon Man.*

The seventies brought a slump in children's book sales, and editors became fussier about the manuscripts they could accept. James Marshall, Lori Segal, Tomie de Paola, and David Macaulay all made contributions to writing that reflected the belief of Margaret Wise Brown that children were looking for emotional climate in their first books and Lucy Sprague Mitchell's advocacy of the celebration of the ordinary in picture book stories.

The sixties and seventies brought a new awareness of children's books that acknowledged their importance in forming ideas and ideals for a lifetime. *Little Black Sambo,* a classic story that children have loved for a century, was reevaluated by adults who looked askance at the stereotypical East Indian child who stars in the story. *The Five Chinese Brothers,* a masterpiece of a story, retold by Claire Huchet Bishop and illustrated in yellow and black by Kurt Wiese, raised outcries from the Chinese community for the stereotypes it perpetuated (see Illustration 1-2). A preponderance of stories about white, middle-class, sub-

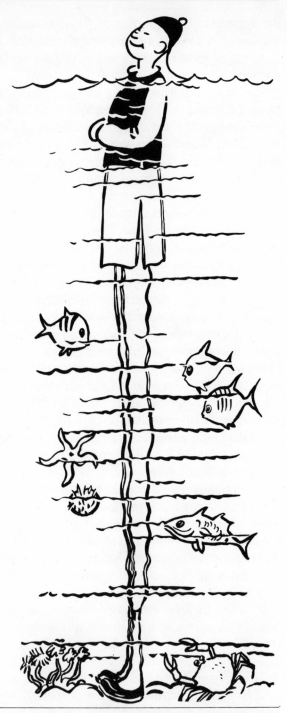

Illustration 1-2.

Author Claire Huchet Bishop and illustrator Kurt Wiese show one of The Five Chinese Brothers *standing up out of the sea in this metaphorical tale exploring the possibilities of the human body.*

urban life, featuring mommies in aprons, daddies with newspapers, raised questions among parents and teachers, librarians and publishers. Shouldn't children's picture books make an effort to avoid the pitfalls that have been identified in this socially conscious era we live in?

The debate rages. *The Little Engine That Could* has enjoyed new popularity as a feminist tract. *Little Black Sambo* has all but disappeared from library shelves, and teachers are torn between the time-tested merit of *The Five Chinese Brothers* as a story and its offensiveness to a significant segment of our population. On the other side of this coin, publishers have gone out of their way to find stories about handicapped children, children facing the problems of a single-parent family, black and Hispanic children, Indians, and little girls who will grow up expecting more from life than aprons and vacuum cleaners. The sixties produced an awareness of a problem, the seventies produced a plethora of possible solutions, and the eighties will see what survives as a contribution and what disappears as a fad.

In the sixties and the seventies, as if in response to children's demand for exciting visuals, the illustrator took center stage, with prolific and popular illustrators writing their own stories as well as illustrating them. This resulted in some delightfully original books—such as William Steig's *Sylvester and the Magic Pebble,* James Marshall's *George and Martha,* and Tomie de Paola's *Nana Upstairs, Nana Downstairs*—but it also resulted in a raft of folk tales, Mother Goose rhymes, and traditional tales wherein the words were used to showcase the illustration. Some illustrators have developed into outstanding writers, including Maurice Sendak and William Kurelek, both artists with a powerful memory—Sendak's *Outside Over There* recalls images if not incidents of his growing up, whereas Kurelek recreated his Canadian boyhood directly and delightfully in *Lumberjack.* But other illustrators are looking outside themselves for good stories, stories that inspire their best work, that lead them in new directions. This is where the writer comes in, especially now that the publishing industry, serving a changing market, is more careful, more conscious of the high standards of what has gone before and less dazzled by new illustration technique for the sake of its novelty.

How a Picture Book Is Put Together

Thus the writer more than ever is a member of a team, just as a screenwriter writes with the director, the cameraman, and the actors always in mind. Understanding the conventions of picture book production is a first step in becoming a member of the picture book team. The

Illustration 1-3.

This colorful jacket illustration for Curious George, *showing "the naughty little monkey" hero hauled away by two firemen, piques the reader's interest without giving away the story.*

illustrator's first contribution is the book's jacket. (Look at *Curious George's*—the simple picture promises high adventure on a childlike scale. See Illustration 1-3.)

The illustrator's influence begins with the jacket. This influence continues from the very first page of your book to the very last. Traditionally, the first page, which is always a single right-hand page, is the half-title page. The only text it bears is the title itself. Its original function was to protect the title page of the book as the binding wore out. With today's sturdy bindings, this is no longer a necessity, and some publishers dispense with it altogether, but it is also considered a graceful element in the art of good bookmaking. It is a fine place to introduce a simple illustration: look at Harry, Gene Zion's dirty dog, in the half-title-page illustration by Margaret Bloy Graham (Illustration 1-4). An

HARRY
the Dirty Dog

Illustration 1-4.

Harry the Dirty Dog is off to a beguiling start with this half-title page, which shows Harry ready for a bath—or is he? The half-title page lists only the title of the book, and it is included in well-designed books as a mood piece to help set the scene, as this engaging and ambiguous illustration does.

Illustration 1-5.

A Chinese-style table contains the vital information of the title page in this illustration by Kurt Wiese. By presenting the information in a visual element the author-artist unifies story and pictures from the very beginning.

enterprising illustrator can use the half-title page to generate excitement and anticipation for your story.

The title page, which follows the half-title page, is included in every book, by law. Besides the title, it gives the names of the author, the illustrator, the publisher, and the publisher's address. An inventive illustrator isn't content simply to find room on the title page for artwork, he tries to make the title an integral part of the picture, to convey if he can the whole spirit of the book. In *You Can Write Chinese* Kurt Wiese has done this with overwhelming success: he has made the block of type into a writing table with a boy leaning over it, leading the young reader to think, "I can write Chinese, too!" (Illustration 1-5.)

The legal details in the copyright notice, which must by law appear either on the title page itself or on its reverse side, are essential for the protection of the author's, illustrator's, and publisher's rights to the book. Tomie de Paola dressed up the copyright page for his young audience by including it in an inconspicuous sign in *Charlie Needs a Cloak,* again demonstrating how the artist's ingenuity can integrate required text into the design of the whole book (Illustration 1-6).

Illustration 1-6.

Copyright information can be a bore to a picture book reader. Here author-artist Tomie de Paola disguises it in a sign and decorates it with a lovable flock of sheep in Charlie Needs a Cloak.

Illustration 1-7.

A dedication page should be something special, as it is in the hands of Alice and Martin Provensen in My Little Hen. *The personal touch is evident in the sweet illustration as well as in the beautifully handwritten inscription.*

for Karen Anna

De Paola included the dedication on the copyright page in this example, but many writers prefer to have the dedication on its own page. Alice and Martin Provensen combine a spot illustration and handwriting on the dedication page of *My Little Hen* (Illustration 1-7). This picture gets the story moving before any of the words written to tell it are read.

These preliminary pages, whose presence is dictated by historical convention and whose content is dictated by law, are really the artist's domain. The author contributes only the title, his name, and the name of the person to whom the book is dedicated—a privilege that is often shared with the illustrator. The illustrator enlivens these pages, called *front matter* in publishing jargon, with appealing pictures so that the reader is led into the story from the moment he opens the book.

When you are planning your book, you will want to allow at least three of your thirty-two pages for this front matter. You may want to allow as many as five pages, depending on the extent to which preliminary illustration can contribute to the mood of your story. In addition, the last page is often an illustration without words, called a *tailpiece* (Illustrations 1-8 and 1-9). An elegant, well-made book does not skimp on the front and back matter any more than an opera does on the overture and finale. The interest in these pages of illustration comes out of the story you have written, and builds up anticipation and excitement in your reader.

Illustration 1-8.

Just as front matter is the overture to a picture book, so the tailpiece on the last single page of the book can be a resounding finale. The three soldiers who introduce the story of Stone Soup *(Illustration 1-8) disappear in the distance in this tailpiece (Illustration 1-9), which closes the story.*

Illustration 1-9.

Pictures pave the way; the kinds of pictures chosen to illustrate your story will affect your young reader's feelings about the story before he has read a word. This is not to suggest that the illustrator takes over the picture book content. Rather, it highlights one of the distinctive qualities of the picture book—the combination of words and visual images. The writer inspires the illustrations which begin the picture book, and the writer sustains the interest in the story.

Anticipating the illustrator's contribution is one of the ways that the picture book writer has to work harder to produce fewer words than other writers. Some details are reflected in both the text and the pictures, while others are shown only in the pictures and still others are mentioned only in the text. The writer becomes a juggler, reinforcing the reader's understanding of the story through pictures in some cases, leaving the pictures to the reader's imagination in other cases. The balance between what is illustrated and what is not is the picture book author's art, and this balance is an individual matter. No two writers approach writing for illustration in the same way.

Compare *The Story of Ferdinand* with Maurice Sendak's *The Sign on Rosie's Door.* In Munro Leaf's tale of an apparently ferocious bull with a pacifist heart, nearly every sentence is illustrated, including the final simple declaration: "He is very happy." *The Sign on Rosie's Door,* on the other hand, has a lot of unillustrated words, such as:

> "First," Lenny explained, "I throw my hat up in the air and then the one who catches it can keep it. Everybody want to play?"
>
> They all shook their heads yes.
>
> "All right," said Alinda.
>
> Lenny threw the hat high into the air and it landed on Rosie's window ledge.

The page on which all this happens has just one illustration.

Both of these stories are aimed at five- and six-year-olds, yet the issue of what is illustrated and what is not is treated very differently. Professionals in the children's book business, including artists, writers, designers, editors, educators, and librarians, recognize that there is a great deal of maneuvering room in the balance between words and pictures. Many prizes are awarded every year for outstanding picture books (a listing is given at the end of the chapter), and each prize reflects a slightly different bias as to what constitutes a successful collaboration of artist and writer, words and pictures.

The different standards and tastes of the experts who judge these awards are an indication of the variety of tastes in the picture book audience—children, parents, librarians, teachers, adult collectors of children's books—assuring the author that there are no hard-and-fast rules for a "good" picture book. What works for one child may not be of interest to another. The picture book writer who writes for the child he knows—whether that child is the child he was or a child he knows very well—is headed in the right direction.

AWARD	GRANTED BY	GIVEN FOR	SOME TYPICAL WINNERS
Caldecott Medal	American Library Association	Best illustrated book	*Sylvester and the Magic Pebble*—William Steig *Make Way for Ducklings*—Robert McCloskey
ALA Notable Books	ALA	Excellence of text and art	*Little Fox Goes to the End of the World*—Ann Tompert
Horn Book Fanfare	*Horn Book* magazine	Enduring excellence	*Fables*—Arnold Lobel
School Library Journal Best Books	SLJ	Originality and reader appeal	*Kate Crackernuts*—K.M. Briggs *The Night Swimmers*—Betsy Byars
AIGA Best Books	American Institute of Graphic Arts	Design and quality manufacturing	*Anno's Alphabet*—Mitsumasa Anno *Handtalk*—Remy Charlip Photo illustrations by George Ancona
New York Times Choice of the Illustrated Children's Books of the Year	*New York Times*	Personalized selection by distinguished panel for excellence and appropriateness of illustration	*Stone and Steel*—Guy Billout *A Child's Christmas in Wales*, illustrated by Edward Ardizzone
Boston Globe/Horn Book		2 prizes: 1 for outstanding text 1 for outstanding illustrations	*The Garden of Abdul Gasazi*—Chris Van Allsburg
Irma Simonton Black Award	Bank Street College	Excellence in children's literature (text and illustrations)	*Gorky Rises*—William Steig

2

Finding Your Place in the Picture

There are three basic kinds of picture books for children. Each has its own characteristics, its own audience, its own authors. This chapter will help you channel your interests and thought processes to create the kind of book you want to write.

The Pigeonholes

The *storybook* is the preschooler's novel, introducing characters who progress through a seductive beginning, and an exciting middle, to a satisfying end. The *informational book* is the preschooler's encyclopedia article, or feature from *Sports Illustrated* or *National Geographic.* It is a clear and comprehensive look at a discrete aspect of life: how a spaceship is launched, where the Apaches lived, what Charles Lindbergh did. The *concept book* is halfway between an essay and an advertisement. Like an essay, it explores an idea, explains how things fit together. Like an advertisement, it "sells" the idea—for instance, the

Illustration 2-1.

In Tana Hoban's Push Pull, Empty Full, *a concept book introducing opposites, the author-photographer contrasts the ideas of "few" and "many." Like all concept books, the distillation of ideas makes the presentation seem deceptively simple.*

multitude of shapes—with the help of pictures. If it's successful, the young reader "buys" the idea, and by the end of the book sees a sphere in a basketball, a rectangle in a tabletop. In Tana Hoban's *Push Pull, Empty Full,* the concept of opposites is explored through contrasting photographs (Illustration 2-1).

All three of these forms overlap. It would be hard to say whether Oliver Selfridge's *All About Mud* is a concept book or an informational book. *Andy: That's My Name* is a concept book that tells a story as well. *Mei Li,* a moving tale of China, is rich in informational details about life in Peking before the Second World War. Is it an informational book or a storybook? It doesn't matter, because it's that rare beast, the storybook that succeeds in conveying information without preaching.

What *does* matter is focusing your interests and talents on the kind of book that is right for you.

The test that follows isn't a scientific survey or a measure of intelligence, but rather a series of questions that should get you to analyze yourself—what you think about, as well as how you think about it. Take it with a grain of salt, but take it: it will narrow down the nearly infinite possibilities in picture book writing and lead you in a direction that is uniquely your own.

What Kind of Book Should You Be Writing?
(A Guide to Finding Your Style)

1. You see a scarlet tanager in the backyard. Do you
   a) wonder why he hasn't flown south?
   b) imagine the conversations he might have with the sparrows and starlings at the feeder?
   c) consider how long he can fly before he has to rest?

2. A child wakes you at night with bad dreams. You talk to him until he's ready to go back to sleep. Do you
   a) tell him about a nightmare you had when you were young that seems silly to both of you now?
   b) create a story about the sandman who overslept and how he woke up just in time to put a little boy to sleep?
   c) describe the animals outside, falling asleep, each in his particular place?

3. You are going on a camping trip. The one thing you don't forget to pack is
   a) a tree identification guide.
   b) a lantern.
   c) a fishing rod.

4. Your reliable husband is twenty minutes late. Do you imagine
   a) he's run into an old friend and they have so much to talk about they forget about the time?
   b) he's found a lost puppy by the side of the road and he has stopped to buy you flowers to convince you to say yes, you can keep him?
   c) there was an accident on the freeway two hours ago, and traffic is backed up for miles?

5. You are alone in a country house on a rainy afternoon. The books accumulated over the years don't seem too promising, but you pick
   a) a du Maurier novel you just loved when you were sixteen.
   b) the thirteenth volume of a turn-of-the-century encyclopedia.
   c) a detective novel from the twenties.

6. You are walking to the store with a child relative you don't see very often. Which direction does the conversation take?
   a) You explain the construction of each building you pass.
   b) You reminisce about the way the street was when you were growing up here.
   c) Between you, you figure out how to get to the store and back without walking on the same side of the street twice.

7. Your mind wanders as you push a child on a swing. The slide catches your eye. Do you
   a) shudder at how scary it was to slide down it the first time?
   b) count the steps to the top and figure out how many feet off the ground that makes it?
   c) wonder how children entertained themselves before playground equipment was invented?

8. You're driving alone on a long trip. Do you
   a) change the station constantly to hear the local stations?
   b) sing to yourself?
   c) drive in silence, keeping an eye on the speedometer, the oil gauge, the odometer, and occasionally the road?

9. You inherit $5,000 from an indulgent great-aunt who stipulated you spend it on yourself. Would you
   a) go on a long trip?
   b) buy a fur coat to see if that will make winter more tolerable?
   c) buy the vacant lot next door because you've always wanted a big garden?

10. The local library wants to start a Saturday morning activity program. Your friend the librarian is pressuring you to contribute your time. Would you
    a) drag armloads of old clothes and clutter from the basement to stage a props-and-costume impromptu production of *Cinderella?*
    b) bring your camera collection and let the kids experiment with different kinds of cameras from your old Brownie to the brand-new Polaroid?
    c) show them twenty things they could do with a piece of string from tricks to knots?

11. You are driving your daughter and her four friends to camp three hours away. You entertain them with
    a) jokes.
    b) reminiscences.
    c) Twenty Questions.

12. Your family gets together for a reunion. Do you join the group playing
    a) touch football on the front lawn?
    b) Risk in the family room?
    c) charades in the living room?

13. You are buying a picture for the wall in your study. Do you choose
    a) a photograph?
    b) an abstract painting?
    c) a classic portrait?

14. When you have a free hour, are you likely to
    a) go for a walk to no place in particular?
    b) attack a crossword puzzle?
    c) finish up a needlepoint pillow?

15. As a cook, you are
    a) quick, but not fancy.
    b) a determined follower of recipes.
    c) a gourmet adventurer.

16. You've baked a loaf of bread to drop off at your new neighbors' after work. Do you wear
    a) the burnoose your cousin just sent you from Haifa?
    b) your jogging suit?
    c) the clothes you wore to work that day?

17. You have just been given a pair of finches. Do you name them
    a) Orville and Wilbur?
    b) Tristan and Isolde?
    c) Darwin and Huxley?

18. If you moved away, would you let your old friends and neighbors know about your move and new address via
    a) a Xeroxed letter?
    b) a formal announcement?
    c) a funny card?

19. Your book has just won first prize in a regional writing competition. You are on your way to the award ceremony. Do you arrive
    a) in a rented limo?
    b) in a station wagon packed with your friends?
    c) alone, in the new sports car you bought with the prize money?

20. The pen you carry is
    a) your grandfather's leaky Mont Blanc.
    b) a stylish felt-tip.
    c) an Eraser-Mate ballpoint.

---

test key

1 — storybook
2 — concept
3 — informational

1. a) 3	6. a) 3	11. a) 2	16. a) 1
b) 1	b) 1	b) 1	b) 3
c) 2	c) 2	c) 3	c) 2
2. a) 2	7. a) 1	12. a) 3	17. a) 3
b) 1	b) 2	b) 2	b) 1
c) 3	c) 3	c) 1	c) 2
3. a) 3	8. a) 2	13. a) 3	18. a) 1
b) 1	b) 1	b) 2	b) 3
c) 2	c) 3	c) 1	c) 2
4. a) 2	9. a) 1	14. a) 3	19. a) 1
b) 1	b) 3	b) 2	b) 3
c) 3	c) 2	c) 1	c) 2
5. a) 1	10. a) 1	15. a) 2	20. a) 1
b) 3	b) 3	b) 3	b) 2
c) 2	c) 2	c) 1	c) 3

If you find yourself in the first category, you are a storyteller, a person with a strong imagination and no embarrassment about sharing it. The second type is more philosophical, interested in ideas, broad generalizations, wide vistas. The third type is the curious person, a collector and lover of facts, the adventurous explorer of the world around him.

The first type is most comfortable with picture storybooks, the second with concept books, the third with information books. If your answers don't fit neatly into categories, don't fret. Versatility is a considerable advantage, and as I mentioned before, picture books certainly don't always fit perfectly into one category or another, either. What we're after here is simply an index to the way your mind works.

The way you think is one handy guide to the kind of book you should write. A second consideration is what interests you. Nonny Hogrogian is a storyteller whose *One Fine Day* won the Caldecott Award. She is also the author of *Homemade Secret Hiding Places,* a how-to book that required the imagination of a storyteller as well as the attention to detail that characterizes the informational picture book writer.

What do you do when you aren't writing picture books? Pauline Watson, an accomplished cook and a trained singer, combined these two hobbies into a singing recipe book called *Cricket's Cookery,* which features, among other amazing combinations, a cookie recipe you can sing to the tune of "Oh, My Darling Clementine." And then consider what you write about when you aren't writing picture books. A detective-story writer who travels to Austria to research a setting might find that this same trip leads him to write a simple biography of the young Mozart. A journalist covering a local Medicare scandal could find material for a storybook about a friendship between a young boy and an old man. A travel writer who covers vacationing in Las Vegas might be inspired to write a concept book about the basic ideas behind probability.

The picture books you write come from your life—your writing life and your nonwriting life. So far, I have described the logical ways of finding a direction; the illogical ones work even better. The picture book is flexible: a sudden insight or a big idea can be structured into a fascinating book. Haris Petie watched her children struggle through the process of learning large numbers. It's an easy thing for adults to understand, but hard to explain. "Bugs!" Petie thought, and created a concept book called *Billions of Bugs* that explains how tens become hundreds and hundreds become thousands in drawings of insects—three hundred no-see-ums, a thousand Monarch butterflies. Similarly, an amusing incident can make great picture book material. When Blanche Dorsky, a nursery school teacher, discovered that her class's pet rabbit's malaise was nothing more than a pregnancy—very upsetting to

Illustration 2-2.

Illustration 2-3.

Great ideas can draw on earlier influences, even when the influence is unconscious. The superficial similarities of George and Martha *(Illustration 2-2) by James Marshall, with Babar and Celeste from* The Story of Babar *(Illustration 2-3) are offset by the deep differences revealed in the styles of the two different books.*

the children, who had thought of the rabbit as Harry—she and the children renamed the rabbit Harriet, then wrote Harriet's story. It became a charming picture book, called *Harry, A True Story.*

Many writers are discouraged from putting their ideas down on paper to submit as picture book manuscripts because it seems as if every good idea for a children's picture book has already been used. One of the most vexing frustrations for editor and author alike is the "it's been done before" problem. Children's interests vary little from generation to generation. They are interested in animals, everyday excitements such as trucks and stoves, relationships with siblings and parents, and monsters who spill milk and keep children awake at night. It would be very difficult to find a children's book subject or approach that is entirely new.

When James Marshall introduced his adorable hippos in the *George and Martha* books (Illustration 2-2)—now a popular series—skeptics pointed out the similarity to the Babar books (Illustration 2-3). At first glance, the resemblance is striking: big gray beasts with pin-point eyes making their way amiably through difficult situations. On closer examination, it is the two series' *dissimilarities* that stand out. Babar is an old-fashioned hero, innocently offering and accepting friendship with a "happily-ever-after" flair. George, his hippopotamus counterpart, is just as friendly, but his good intentions are thwarted by modern realities. In a matter as simple as shoes, we see how Marshall's hippo faces problems that never confront Babar. When Babar, being a jungle elephant, arrives in Paris shoeless, a dear old lady buys him shoes and spats. George, being a city hippo, has a pair of shoes, and when his friend Martha makes him some pea soup he doesn't like, he pours the soup in his shoe—and gets caught. The surface similarity bothered adults initially, but contemporary children saw humor and compatibility in George and Martha that took them one step beyond the world populated by Babar and Celeste.

Similar characters are inevitable, and so are similar situations. Tomie de Paola had experimented for a while with a picture book about weaving and spinning before he hit upon the idea of a bumbling shepherd making a cloak for himself from the fleece of his unwilling pet sheep. *Charlie Needs a Cloak* seemed so original and funny to the editors when it was submitted to Prentice-Hall that we didn't think it needed to be judged in comparison to other books about the process of wool-gathering and weaving. The marketing people were nervous because Elsa Beskow had created *Pelle's New Suit* thirty years before, and what twentieth-century children's collection would need *two* picture books about wool? We agonized over the similarities until we began to consider the differences. One fundamental difference was the change in attitudes toward "men's work" and "women's work" in that thirty-year gap. While Pelle exchanged men's chores—painting, chopping, hammering—for the weaving, dyeing, cutting, and sewing of his new suit, which are traditionally assigned to women, the contemporary Charlie took on these latter tasks himself.

The enormous popularity of *George and Martha* and *Charlie Needs a Cloak* is a reminder that the children's book writer is working within a tradition. Originality is no guarantee of success. You may submit the only picture book ever written about open-heart surgery or George Eliot's girlhood, and find that it's turned down for lack of interest. If you submit a good-night book, a birthday book, or a little-animal-who-runs-away story, it may be turned down, too, but it won't be for lack of audience interest. Carbon copies are of course to be avoided, but a manuscript that builds on a traditional topic in an original way will be welcomed, just as a variation on a theme is welcomed in a sonata.

When your manuscript is rejected because the idea has already found its way into print, consider the matter carefully. What's new about your approach? What's unique about your characterization? Check with the *Subject Guide to Books in Print,* and study the competition. There is, as the expression goes, always room for one more—if it makes its own contribution. The demand for material on certain subjects central to childhood is the same generation after generation. In his sensitive picture book *Johnny Mapleleaf,* published in the forties, Alvin Tresselt addressed the question of dying—a question children wonder about and adults would rather not discuss. A leaf grows and falls in a natural way that is both reassuring and factual. Twenty years later, Barbara Borack addressed the same subject with a different setting in a storybook, *Someone Small.* Her story revolves around a parakeet who is a young girl's companion while the rest of the family seems wrapped up in the new baby. When the parakeet dies, the heroine is able to accept her younger sister's arrival in a story that in its parallel relationships has the richness of a novel. It was written for a child with slightly different concerns than the reader of *Johnny Mapleleaf.* A few years later, Judith Viorst wrote *The Tenth Good Thing about Barney,* the story of a pet cat who dies, which can be categorized as a concept book. No one dismissed this sensitive story, which explains a pet's death as part of the life cycle of the world, as a repeat of the same theme. Viorst offered a new viewpoint, a lively set of characters, and a contemporary setting that made her book unique. These three books on the same subject are complementary, each with its special approach.

Great minds, as Alexander Pope pointed out, do think alike. No matter how careful an editor or author is to make sure a picture book offering is unique, there is no guarantee that somebody isn't writing the same book at the same time you are. Many authors feel that when they submit their manuscripts to a publisher they are making it possible for their ideas to be stolen. Publishers don't steal ideas, but the long arm of coincidence creates some amazing circumstances! Jean Burt Polhamus, a San Diego writer who specializes in dinosaurs, and Syd Hoff, a New York writer who specializes in humorous writing for children, collided head on a few seasons ago, when they had the same good idea at the same time. While Polhamus was polishing up her manuscript on the West Coast, Hoff was working on his on the East Coast, and in the fall of 1975, two picture books called *Dinosaur Dos and Don'ts* appeared. Both were funny books full of pictures of naughty dinosaurs in outrageous situations. Did it hurt either book? Ironically, the answer is no, because the simultaneous appearance of the two books gave reviewers something extra to talk about: both books were widely reviewed and have survived to sell very well.

"I spent five years in solitary confinement writing *Outside Over There*," Maurice Sendak admits, "which has 351 words. I don't have a new idea." The picture book author is looking for new angles and approaches, not new ideas. The experiences of childhood are so similar that the picture book writer's primary job is not finding an unexplored subject, as a journalist's might be, but rather finding a sympathetic subject, one that he has something to say about that children can relate to and hear. Your audience's interests have been researched, diagnosed, discussed, and agreed upon: finding your place in the picture depends on focusing on yourself and your interests. The test of a good subject for a picture book is the interest it holds for you. The more interested you are in what you are writing about, the more depth and originality you can convey in the small space you have to work in.

"Childhood," mystery writer P.D. James says, "is the one prison from which there's no escape, the one sentence from which there's no appeal. We all serve our time." The limitations of the childhood experience are what make it universally interesting; freed from the endless search for a new subject, the writer is able to concentrate on individual expression, personal insight, and specific memory, the hallmarks of great writing.

3

The State of the Art

Who is the children's book illustrator? In the past fifty years, children's book illustration has been elevated into a craft, a profession, an art that appeals to practitioners from many artistic disciplines. Greeting card artists, portraitists, photographers, and print-makers are turning to children's picture book illustration as a medium that allows full expression and the special reward of winning a child to pictures for a lifetime. As the writer writes, he should be mindful of the kinds of illustrations that have been popular in the past, the illustrations that reflect current tastes, and the trends that are ripe for revival. And the writer must guess, along with the rest of the publishing community, what the new directions for children's book illustrations will be.

Pictures in children's storybooks started out two hundred years ago as crude woodcuts, often afterthoughts placed any old where to break up the text into child-size pieces. Some of the classic children's books have downright ugly illustrations, but it can be argued that the spunk of Helen Bannerman's pictures for *Little Black Sambo* has contributed to that book's lasting appeal. It's hard, but not impossible, to find this kind of unpolished art in books published today: certainly some illustrators bring a childlike quality to their work. Nicole Rubel, in *Rotten Ralph,* reveals an amusing and congenial spontaneity that is no happy accident—it comes from years of formal training. In *George's Store* and *Elvira Everything* Frank Asch draws pictures we all are convinced we could duplicate—until we try to imitate his inspired madness, executed with quirky line.

Why don't all children's book illustrations have this childlike quality, since children respond to it so favorably? The pat answer is that children's book illustrations reflect the wide diversity of commercial and fine art in general. The time-tested, professionally evaluated conclusion is that simplicity and directness appeal most to the youthful eye.

There are psychological studies which show that children of two and three respond far more strongly to primary colors than they do to pastels; that changes in hair styles and clothing that are not described in the text disconcert beginning readers; that children count on pictures to help them "read" the story. Children of five and six are very resourceful at utilizing pictures to decipher jumps in the story, and as children become more experienced in reading and looking at picture books, they come to appreciate subtle tones and careful detail in the illustrations as well as in the story. Because of this difference in response of two- and three-year-olds and six- and seven-year-olds, many educators believe that children of the picture book age—ages two to eight—should begin with books that feature illustrations of familiar objects a child has seen for himself. Then he will be ready to accept more fanciful pictures of far-off places and imaginary characters.

All these findings support more and more illustrated books for children. Picture books cover a five- or six-year span in the child's life, and these diverse findings of child psychologists and teachers support books tailored to certain age groups, special interests, and different approaches. This is good news for the illustrator because it means that there is always room for a new edition of a favorite fairy tale, and it is good news for the writer because it points out the ever-present need for new material on contemporary topics and individual areas of interest.

Children's book illustrations, to the extent that they *are* similar to one another, owe a great deal to the development of printing technology. When a color picture is submitted to a publisher, he sends it to a color separator. The color separator has a camera with a set of filters, and he takes at least four pictures of the artwork—one for the yellow, one for the red, one for the blue, and one for the black—to create color plates. One of a printer's biggest problems is to place the four plates precisely on top of one another, in a process that is called *registration*. Pictures in which the color and lines look blurry are the fault of poor registration of the four different plates as they go through the press. One of the easiest ways to control this problem is to include a base cartoon drawing with a strong black holding line which, coloring-book style, is filled in with color. This strong line helps the pressman control the registration of the different colors through the printings of thousands and thousands of books on high-speed presses. Since this style pleases children as well as printers, it has dominated the American approach to illustration.

The changes that artists have discovered and developed within this general "cartoon" form are fascinating. William Steig, who is known for the *New Yorker* drawings he has created for decades, uses a cartoon line in *Sylvester and the Magic Pebble,* enriched with luminous color. Roger Duvoisin, who is noted for his advertising art, which is also done in cartoon style for newspaper reproduction, drew illustrations for *Petunia* and *White Snow Bright Snow* with a strong delineation of brightly colored areas. Emily McCully, in *When Violet Died,* uses her line as almost a shorthand, creating an emotional mood without any visual clutter. Bernard Waber, in *Lyle, Lyle, Crocodile,* has an idiosyncratic line that is warm and funny; he uses color to highlight areas of interest. Rosemary Wells, in *Benjamin and Tulip* and *Miranda's Pilgrims,* is original in her use of color and downright daring in her creation of space and perspective.

Some illustrators have used limited color very successfully. Ingrid Fetz, in *What's Good for a Six-Year-Old?* by William Cole, crosshatches her base line so skillfully that the two-color illustrations alternate with four-color illustrations without being jarring. Marcia Brown, in *Stone Soup,* uses a brown base line highlighted with red to create a steam of the soldiers' soup, the pink on the peasants' faces, and the evening in a French town—visions many of us would expect to require a full palette to be reproduced. Robert Lawson, who became known for his writing with *Rabbit Hill,* started out as an illustrator of Munro Leaf's books, *Wee Gillis* and *The Story of Ferdinand.* Here his simple pen-and-ink illustrations communicate pastoral serenity and big-city excitement without any color at all. In *Andy and the Lion,* by James Daugherty, the colorful story is told with precisely sequential pictures. The author-artist's line drawings are so animated that the limited color is unnoticeable.

Yet color appeals to the young eye, especially in this age of color television and technicolor movies. Robert McCloskey creates a one-color book—appropriately enough, that color is blue—in *Blueberries for Sal.* In *The Five Hundred Hats of Bartholomew Cubbins,* Dr. Seuss works in two colors—black and red—to tell the story of a little boy with a red hat. The young reader never loses sight of that bright red hat as it constantly replaces itself in this magical cumulative tale.

Applying additional colors to the base-line cartoon brings out inventiveness in illustrators. Shirley Hughes delineates her characters distinctly, but she uses color adventurously to create a living, breathing reality in *David and Dog* and *George the Babysitter.* Taro Yashima, who can create the illusion of rain better than any artist in the children's book field, uses his line as a starting point and takes off with color, in *Umbrella* and *Crow Boy.* Don Freeman, in *Corduroy,* applies color cheerfully to his cartoon illustrations, but in *Pet of the Met* he takes the technique a step further and applies both blocks of solid color and shadings in muted color to create mood and character.

All of these styles have evolved from the basic line approach of the cartoon. Other illustrators have concentrated on conveying shapes without guiding lines. The realism of Holling C. Holling's nonfiction picture books, including *Minn of the Mississippi* and *Seabird,* is achieved through a combination of small line drawings reproduced in black and white to explain technical details, and stunning paintings occupying a full page to convey the excitement and mood of his subject. Illustrating fiction for young children at the same time Holling was illustrating non-fiction—before the Second World War—was Clement Hurd, whose illustrations grace *Goodnight Moon* and *The Runaway Bunny,* both best-selling picture books by Margaret Wise Brown. Sun-filled exteriors and cozy interiors are built on the book page without any holding line at all. In *Fortunately,* Remy Charlip fills the page with shapes without the aid of a cartoon line, and taking this technique one step further are collage artists Helen Sewall in *The First Thanksgiving* and Ezra Jack Keats in *Pet Show!* They use the texture and color of the collage to delineate their shapes with a minimum of holding lines. Adrienne Adams in *Hansel and Gretel* paints her page completely, creating a seamless web of place as she draws the dark forest, the cloudy blue sky, and the sunny scenes of the happy ending to this classic fairy tale.

Here, and on the following pages, I have mentioned illustrators not because they are typical but because they have made important and original contributions to the development of children's picture book illustration, using various media to communicate various moods. As you write, you might want to look over the selection of illustrations and find the kind of illustration that best suits your story. Think about how your word pictures "look," and imagine your story illustrated by a Sendak, an Ungerer, or an Adams. Does the dimension the illustrator adds change the message you are conveying? Is there one illustrator whose work seems right for your writing? Allow yourself to wonder why, and imagine how many different ways your manuscript could be illustrated using various approaches to color, line, and composition.

Gaining a thorough familiarity with picture books and with the way illustrations work with words is part of the fun of this area of writing. Jane Yolen, a writer whose work has been illustrated by many different artists, has a collection of examples from each artist. This reminder of the diversity of her own work is a source of inspiration and pleasure to her. Steven Kellogg, who writes his own stories, such as *Can I Keep Him?,* also illustrates the work of others, and finds that this is a fascinating challenge to him as an artist. As you review your own story, try to imagine how you would like to see it illustrated, and consider the possibilities seriously.

In no other field, except perhaps moviemaking, is the writer's appreciation of the contributions of others—including the editor and designer, but most important, the illustrator—more crucial to the writer's success. Cynthia Basil, the author of three picture books, including *How Ships Play Cards* and *Nail Heads and Potato Eyes,* feels that her success in developing her ideas for publication hinges on her ability to think in picture book terms. As the art director of picture books, she admits that she "planned the book for thirty-two pages, understood the limitations of the illustrations and the right amount of words per page, almost instinctively." It is this sixth sense that causes her writing to flow smoothly from page to page, spread to spread, and finally from cover to cover. You can develop an instinct for what will work in a piece of picture book writing by studying the picture books in your library very carefully. You might want to start with the suggestions for further reading at the close of this book. Approach this study not as an exercise in blind appreciation, but one of problems and solutions.

In *The Runaway Bunny,* for instance, Clement Hurd's "problem" is how to let the child exercise his own imagination at the same time he experiences the more developed imagination of the artist through the illustrations. In this book, the "solution" is the appearance of small, suggestive black-and-white illustrations on the text pages chronicling the conversation of the little bunny who wants to run away, and his mother who is inventive in the ways she will follow him. "If you become a fish in a trout stream," says his mother, "I will become a fisherman and I will fish for you." The illustration—done in simple black and white—shows mother bunny about to don her fishing gear. But— turn the page—there she is decked out in hip boots casting with a carrot on the end of her line where the would-be runaway bunny leaps for it, as any good bunny would.

In *Song of the Swallows,* Leo Politi's "problem" is the alternating color in the book. For reasons of economy, the book alternates two-color spreads with four-color spreads. In this Caldecott-winning picture book, the author-artist uses this limitation as an advantage by placing close-ups of the leading characters and details of the natural landscape on the two-color pages. On the four-color pages, he presents his reader with commanding views of the swallows in flight and panoramas of the mission town in which the young hero Juan lives.

Every picture book offers similar exercises of problem-posing and solution-finding. A critical study of illustration will aid your writing—and also give you hours of pleasure, for illustration is a fascinating art.

PART TWO

PICTURE PERFECT, LETTER PERFECT

4

Picture Book People: Characters and Characterization

Do you know Katy? She's a tractor who has been put out to pasture by the town she has served all her life. She's considered obsolete, but Katy is a strong and solid character who waits for her time to shine. When a winter storm takes her little town by surprise, Katy chugs to the rescue as an efficient snowplow. Katy's saga speaks to the child who has had to wait in line to go down the slide or be pushed in the swing, to the child who is impatient for her turn at Show and Tell, and to the child who has watched three big brothers wear the skates before she gets her chance to skim across the ice. How did Virginia Lee Burton, the author of *Katy and the Big Snow,* think of personifying a tractor, of all things? The mother of two boys, she became fascinated with their fascination with machinery. With a leap of imagination, this writer brought a hunk of rusty iron to life. Her curiosity led her beyond machinery to create an appealing personality.

Although the story contains a lesson about helping others, Hardie Gramatky, the author of *Little Toot,* did not set out to write a tract about responsibility. Gramatky, a talented and prolific New York artist, often gazed out his studio window at the tugboats on the Hudson River. From those apparently idle hours came Little Toot. Watching the tugs from afar, Gramatky pondered the peculiar life of a tugboat. Delving deeper and deeper, he created a young tugboat with a winning smile with whom generations of children have identified.

Writers who bring inanimate objects to life often start by observing people. What people do, how they react, when they talk, when they're silent, are so intriguing to these observers-turned-writers that they never forget what they've seen and heard. Years later, sitting at their typewriters, they put these years of observation down on paper as exactingly as a legal scholar citing cases.

If writers are so interested in people, why do they write stories about tugboats and mooses and cabooses and monkeys and elves? The child's own lively imagination is the most compelling, the most important, and the most delightful reason the writer has for indulging in fantasy. The child hasn't yet learned to scorn imagery, to suspect fantasy, to value hard, cold facts over truth-conveying symbols. He is a poet still, open to words of wisdom from owls, trees, and people equally, to truthful situations dealing with mice or men or minibikes. What an irresistible opportunity—to write for an audience at once so receptive to the real world and to the world of the imagination! Then, too, think of how diverse the picture book audience is, and what a short time the author has to capture its attention. An adult novelist has fifty years of novel-reading time to reach his audience. There are times when an adult reader will pick up *The Brothers Karamazov;* at other times, *Hawaii* will have more appeal. The picture book writer has only the years between ages two and eight to captivate his reader, so he is going to use *every* trick in the book to get attention. A universally appealing character is the best insurance.

Studies show that children don't like to read about children who are younger than they are; that girls will read about boys, but boys are reluctant to read about girls. Advocacy groups further limit human characterization: some people think that only blacks can write about black children, that only women can write about the experience of girlhood. What's a writer to do if he wants to write about people without alienating this group or that? The time-tested solution is to write about people in disguise. Aesop discovered this more than two thousand years ago when he collected fables about the fox, the stork, and the city mouse. H.A. Rey knew it when he introduced Curious George, "a naughty little monkey" who is as much a kid as any human could be.

Three Great Mice

Let's take mice, favorite human substitutes in children's books. There is a host of possible reasons mice are so popular: they never grow beyond small; they are timid yet mischievous; they are helpless prey for larger animals. No wonder children find identification with mice so natural! Three great mice in literature for young children are Edna Miller's Mousekin, a white-footed mouse who lives in the woods (Illustration 4-1); Leo Lionni's Frederick, a more suburban mouse who lives on the edge of the human world and has some outstanding human values (Illustration 4-2); and that nameless Mouse who stars in Robert Kraus's *Whose Mouse Are You?* (Illustration 4-3). This endearing rodent has none of the qualities of the mice we're familiar with, but he is a mouse through and through.

First, look at the way these three mice are drawn. You can almost feel Mousekin's soft fur as you look at the watercolor rendering of him; Frederick looks more like a toy mouse, but he is as cute as a but-

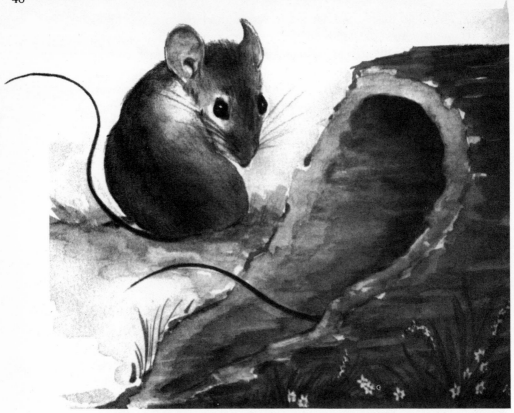

Illustration 4-1.
Mousekin, naturally mouselike, is so realistically drawn by author Edna Miller that the reader is tempted to reach out and stroke the little creature, in this drawing from Mousekin Finds a Friend.

ton; Mouse is more like a kid in need of orthodontia than a biologically correct mouse.

Edna Miller has written a series of books about Mousekin, who lives in the woods behind her house in Warwick, New York. Miller has created Mousekin directly from the natural model—she captures a mouse for each book to study him (and spoils him with apples and raisins while he lives in his comfortable cage). When the book is finished, she sets him free. Every detail of Mousekin's environment is scrupulously researched, and he meets only the animals he might encounter in real life.

"I identify with mice," the elegant author admits. "They are timid, and have every reason to be, because they are so small. Children share my empathy with a mouse's plight in the big woods."

In book after book, Mousekin's innocence gets him into trouble. He confronts life-or-death situations without even realizing that he's in

Illustration 4-2.

*The hero of Leo Lionni's Frederick
looks more like a toy mouse than
the real thing. His stance and expression
speak to young children in search
of a character they can identify with.*

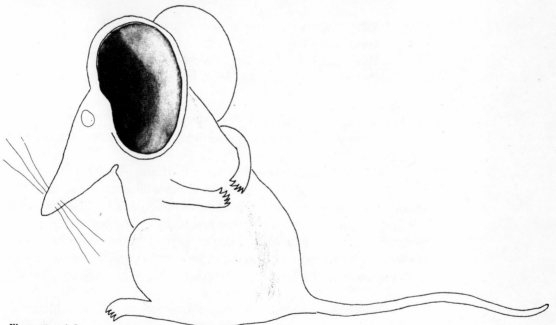

Illustration 4-3.

The lonely little mouse Jose Aruego has drawn to illustrate Robert Kraus's Whose Mouse Are You?
engages the reader with his boyish posture and endearing big ears.

trouble, because he is too small to have any perspective. Through the writer's artistry, the young reader has the perspective Mousekin lacks. Any five-year-old can tell you that this little mouse counts on his luck too much. When Mousekin escapes from the family trailer into the Arizona desert, children invariably cry: "Look out, Mousekin!" Children identify with Mousekin because he has all the traits of the gentle but curious child who never really stands out, in the classroom or in the neighborhood.

Leo Lionni's Frederick, on the other hand, is a standout mouse. Frederick's characterization pays only lip service to normal mouse activities. He is a member of a "chatty family of field mice" who spend their summers collecting food for the winter. Not Frederick: he sits quietly by, gathering sun rays, colors, and words for the drab winter ahead. We get to know and like Frederick, even though we are quick to assume that he is a lazy boy with a clever excuse for not helping out. When winter comes, Frederick takes center stage as a visionary, telling stories, calling up colors, reminding the family of the warmth of spring and summer sunshine.

Lionni saves the story from becoming a ho-hum pitch for creativity with a surprise ending. After Frederick recites his remarkable poem:

> Who scatters snowflakes? Who melts the ice?
> Who spoils the weather? Who makes it nice?
> Who grows the four-leaf clovers in June?
> Who dims the daylight? Who lights the moon?

his father marvels, "Frederick, you are a poet!"

"I know it," Frederick replies with a blush to accompany this silly rhyme.

Robert Kraus's mouse in *Whose Mouse Are You?* is far removed from the real-life Mousekin Edna Miller observes and the mouse-boy Lionni devises. This cartoon mouse could be a man or a moose, you think, until you realize how skillfully the author has incorporated mouse traits to tell his story of helping others. "Whose mouse are you?" the story begins, as the author addresses the lonely mouse peeping up from the bottom of the page. "Nobody's mouse," Mouse replies.

After this irresistible opening, the author reveals that Mouse *is* somebody's mouse, just as *every* reader is somebody's child. The much-needed but hard-to-swallow message of sharing with others is conveyed in fewer than fifty words, as Mouse rescues his family—he's a brave little mouse!—and then allows them to pamper him as a reward—he's a sweet little mouse as well!

The great people you meet in picture books are often animals, and it's interesting to consider why Babar is an elephant, Curious George is a monkey, Harry is a dog, and Peter is a rabbit. Judicious selection is a primary factor in the successful transformation of animals and objects—tractor, tugboat, lighthouse—into picture book stars.

Real People

But if you find this route is not for you, that you'd like to face the music and write about people, you have taken on a different but equally difficult task. It *can* work, as *The Sign on Rosie's Door, One Morning in Maine,* and *Sam, Bangs, and Moonshine* attest, but the failures number in the hundreds of thousands, published and unpublished. If there's a secret to success, it might be found in Evaline Ness's remarks on the gray area between imagination and lies:

> I remembered me (as a child) as a liar, and a profitable one. My lies had a way of coming true. Three of them got me a piano, a telephone, and ballet lessons. The shabby misplaced child of my drawing became Sam, who told lies. The baby kangaroo got in the story because of a newspaper article, and I added the cat because I have one.

Like Sendak and McCloskey, Ness wrote about what she knew best: herself. Sendak drew on his childhood memories of Brooklyn, McCloskey on observations of his own child. Many writers make the mistake of writing about children they don't and never did know. Thinking that your own life is of no interest to others is a critical error. The people who write firsthand have a tremendous advantage over secondhand writers.

But the character doesn't have to be faithfully autobiographical in order to succeed with children. Ludwig Bemelmans, the creator of Madeline, was never a schoolgirl in a French convent. But as the son of a noted hotelier, he did know what it was like to be the center of attention for both staff and guests. He invented the spunky Madeline, the kind of child who can exploit adult attention—Miss Clavel's in this case—to win the approval of other children. It worked for Madeline, just as it had for Bemelmans.

The story of Madeline brings up the question of supporting characters in a picture book. Writers for children do not faithfully recreate the family scene but they do explore the world of parents and parent substitutes in the books they write. Miss Clavel and Dr. Cohn illustrate the most important supporting cast of all—parent substitutes. Marie

Hall Ets's classic fantasy *In the Forest* concerns a small boy conjuring up an imaginary group of animal friends. The arrival of a real presence, his father, makes the imaginary animals disappear. The father's role in the story is unobtrusive but crucial.

Where the Wild Things Are and *Peter Rabbit* feature background mothers, for a very good reason. Children thrill to independent adventures, but they like to know that there is some caring adult in the background. The silent presence of the parent serves two purposes: it roots the story in reality, and it makes the adventure (Peter Rabbit's foray into McGregor's garden, and Max's trip to the land of the monsters) safer. The best part of a trip, we all know, is coming home again.

Brothers and sisters, schoolyard bullies, best friends, and other children are other important supporting characters. The child reader is familiar with the relationships that these characters bring to the main character's development, so empathy and identification come more easily. *Show, don't tell!* is a universal editorial admonition; the clever writer looks for supporting characters whose roles don't have to be explained to be recognized. *A Bargain for Frances* is a cautionary tale about a badger named Frances, who believes her best friend's self-serving half-truths. Frances learns to be a little less gullible in this hilarious story. What makes it possible for author Russell Hoban to convey his message is his keen observation of childhood's friendships.

So far, we have explored animals-as-people and people-as-people. Mixing human characters with nonhuman is a tricky business. Two successful examples are *Peter Rabbit* and *Curious George*. Mr. McGregor and the man in the yellow hat are strictly supporting characters, and their appearance does not conflict with the anthropomorphization of the human substitute.

One popular combination of people and inanimate objects is a child and a toy that's endowed with human qualities. In *The Velveteen Rabbit* by Margery Williams, the toy rabbit is the star of the story, and the little boy who loves him is a presence but not a personality. In *The Story of Bangwell Putt*, Mariana tells the story of a little doll who lives in a museum. Her owner is named Clarissa and is described as a blind child, but she does not figure in the doll's adventures. In these stories, the toy takes on human emotions and actions, just as animals do in animal stories. As soon as a writer introduces a human child into his story, he has to be consistent in his characterizations. Consider *Harry the Dirty Dog*. Harry, a dog who hates to take baths, is a pet, but also a member of the family. He has thought processes and pursues activities characteristic of an adventurous boy. The author even gives him a human name. The young reader identifies with both Harry, a dog, and Harry's owners, who are also children.

Stories where fantasy and reality meet require extremely delicate handling. Young children accept—and love—fantasy, but they need clarity. Confusion between the world around them and the world between the covers of a book is more than unsettling; it can be deeply disturbing. In *Where the Wild Things Are,* Maurice Sendak handles the jump from the child's family life to his internal life in a particularly effective way. Talking animals are generally accepted—as long as they talk to one another, rather than to people in realistic situations. After reading about a girl's conversation with a horse, a child could logically suppose that the horse down the street might be able to talk. If combining fantasy with reality is your thing, it's probably best to write for older children, who are less literal in their interpretation.

Consistency is the hobgoblin of little minds only when it is foolish, and there is nothing foolish about respecting the clarity a child requires to understand a new cast of characters. This does not limit your choice of characters—they can be fantastical, realistic, comic, sad, or high-tech, as long as they live in a single world, not requiring shifts from reality to imagination. The picture book is a vehicle for taking the child wherever he wants to go: many children build imaginary characters on the most realistic stories, or see parallels in daily life to the most fantastical picture book character. The very simplicity, the Aristotelian unity, of your characters and their settings creates a stage for the child to develop his own dramas.

Because the picture-book-age child is so inexperienced, exotic characters are a dime a dozen. Anyone who isn't a member of the family or a denizen of the neighborhood is as new and exciting as any fantasy creature. Other cultures, other countries, other times are fascinating. Tasha Tudor's lovely explorations of New England life at the turn of the century are as foreign as an episode of *Star Wars.* But in the same way a child likes to hear the same song over and over, to play the same games, to enjoy routines like grocery shopping and going to the gas station that adults find a little tedious, so the child *needs* the security of familiar characters in his beginning books.

5

Picture Book Plotting: Surprise and Satisfaction

Fiction or nonfiction, folktale or contemporary story, a picture book must be a thriller. Astonishment unfolds in astonishing ways in a picture book: the repetition with a twist in *The Three Little Pigs* (Illustration 5-1), the slow and steady building up to a bang in *Drummer Hoff*, the delicious exploration of the ordinary in *Goodnight Moon*. The picture book's brevity and simplicity demand an extra-strong structure. A novelist can spend three paragraphs describing the landscape without losing his reader; the picture book writer has no such luxury. The journalist can devote thousands of words to background; the picture book writer has to get on with his story.

Plotting a picture book is surprisingly difficult. The tough stan-

Well, he huffed, and he puffed
and he huffed and he puffed
and he huffed and he puffed.

But he could *not* blow the house in.

Illustration 5-1.
Paul Galdone's retelling of The Three Little Pigs *is simple storytelling at its best. Here the wolf huffs and puffs in an electrifying close-up that signals the climax of the story.*

dards include starting at an involving point, building up to a climax in carefully measured steps, and ending with a note of satisfaction, for reassurance, and of surprise, for excitement.

The picture book plot is successful only if its foundations are carefully laid. A standard picture book has a mere twenty-seven pages of text. In those twenty-seven pages, the writer has to establish a beginning, build up to a middle, and wind down to an end. If a writer allots a third of his book to the beginning, another third to the middle, and the final third to the ending, he has only ten pages, on the average, for each of the three parts. Ten pages, five double-page spreads, not much more than fifteen sentences, is scant space. The plot of a picture book leaves no room for error.

Getting Started

A writer chooses a particular starting point so that what happens next will follow from it.

> The sun is tired. It goes down the sky into the drowsy hills. The sunflowers lean. They fall asleep to dream of tomorrow's sun.
> The moon is up!

Janice May Udry begins *The Moon Jumpers* before the action starts, quietly establishing mood and setting the stage for the mysterious joys of staying out after dark on a summer night.

"You and the monster are in the middle of the maze. How fast can you get out?" Jane Sarnoff and Reynold Ruffins ask their readers, ensuring a sense of involvement first thing, in their *Monster Riddle Book.* "Danny sucked his thumb," Kathryn Ernst tells her readers on the first page of *Danny and His Thumb,* immediately capturing the attention of a young thumb-sucker.

However a picture book begins, its effectiveness hinges on the immediacy of its message. A character, a puzzle, an activity: these are the kinds of attention-getters that the author wants to feature on his first page. Your aim is to astonish, baffle, tickle, even shock your reader—to hook him at the start. As you plan the opening of your story, force yourself to be more adventurous than you really think is wise. By consciously overstepping the bounds of logic, you can work backward to describe a situation that commands attention without being ridiculous (unless you want it to be!).

Keep in mind when you start your story that there will be explaining to do later. You want to keep that explaining to a minimum, so you must craft a beginning from a good starting point. Robert

McCloskey's *Make Way for Ducklings* (Illustration 5-2) plunges right into the story:

> Mr. and Mrs. Mallard were looking for a place to live. But every time Mr. Mallard saw what looked like a nice place, Mrs. Mallard said it was no good. There were sure to be foxes in the woods or turtles in the water, and she was not going to raise a family where there might be foxes or turtles. So they flew on and on.

Illustration 5-2.

In Make Way for Ducklings, *Robert McCloskey brings Mr. and Mrs. Mallard to Boston in this delightful bird's-eye illustration of the Public Garden. The birds' direction leads the reader into the story that follows.*

The unanswered questions about the past—how these two ducks met, where they are coming from, how long they've been looking, why they disagree about the right spot—that this curiosity-arousing beginning provokes keep the reader turning the pages. In McCloskey's beginning, the ducks flapping high in the sky arrest the reader's eye. Where will they land? he wonders, and turns the page to find out. Nothing extraneous appears here, but nothing essential is left out.

The Dangerous Middle—Don't Flag!

Once you've selected a starting point—and no rule says that this has to happen before you forge ahead with the first draft of your story—your next hurdle is sustaining interest as your story progresses. In *Andy and the Lion*, Andy and his dog, Prince, are on the way home from the library. They encounter a mysterious blob, with his back turned:

> It looked very queer. [page turn]
> Andy and Prince crept up cautiously to investigate. [page turn]
> It moved!

A picture book writer needs to be mindful of the tricks of his trade in order to keep the story moving along. Daugherty's exquisite timing in the excerpt above is a masterful example of suspensefulness. Since simplicity is your ultimate aim, you will want to consider how repetition, rhyme, refrains, contrasts, and accumulations can help you achieve it. These techniques work to keep distractions of setting, complexities of character, and actions covering a long period of time within the bounds of your reader's comprehension and attention span.

In *Rain Makes Applesauce*, Julian Scheer *repeats* the absurd title to remind the reader of the framework of his nonsense. In *The Story of Zachary Zween*, Mabel Watts uses *rhyme* to tell the story of a little boy who has to come to terms with always being the last:

> And who came last?
> Poor Zachary Zween—
> So envious that his face turned green!
> Yes, Zachary Zween got most upset
> And angry at the alphabet!

Contrast is the tool James Cressey uses in *Fourteen Rats and a Ratcatcher*. The ratcatcher solves the problem of the old lady's rat-infested house by making a deal with the rats that they will remain "as quiet as mice." Every action in this complex but easy-to-follow book is shown on the left-hand page from the old lady's viewpoint and on the facing page from the rats'. The tightly organized structure points up the conflict and resolution of the plot.

Accumulation is a favorite device in picture book plotting. In *The Seed the Squirrel Dropped*, Haris Petie uses the familiar rhyme scheme and ever-growing structure of "This Is the House That Jack Built" to show the life cycle of a cherry tree.

As important as structure is to picture book plots, it is only a framework for good writing. The introduction of other elements—a pause in the story for a descriptive detail, a conversation that alters the pace, a twist of the plot, the internal dialogue of a character thinking a situation through for himself—makes the difference between a lifeless formula and a living, breathing story.

In *Pope Leo's Elephant,* John Lawrence *interrupts* his exciting factual tale about Leofante, the King of Portugal's gift to Pope Leo five hundred years ago, to show the great artist Raphael sketching and painting a portrait of the exotic beast. Far from detracting from the flow of action, this small detail, by fixing the story more firmly in its historical context, makes it more memorable.

Conversation is another device to heighten the suspense as a character heads toward the culmination of a story, slowing the pace so that the young reader can relish the inevitable outcome. In *A Birthday for Frances,* Russell Hoban shows how Frances's lack of willpower may spoil the birthday present she has purchased for her little sister. Clutching the candy bar, Frances discusses with her father her certainty that she will enjoy it more than her sister. By slowing the plot down at this point, Hoban is then able to surprise the reader. We are sure that Frances is going to devour her birthday present, but as the conversation continues, her father gently offers to keep the candy bar for Frances. The twist in the plot is beautifully orchestrated; the conversation allows the writer to change the key of his story without jarring the reader.

Plotting is always dependent on the characterization. The reader gets to know a character first, and becomes interested in what he does second. *Motivation* is one of the important ways a writer can keep his reader's interest during the middle of any picture book. Motivations for young children can be basic and still be very effective. In *Pet Show!* Ezra Jack Keats shows little Archie yearning to win a pet show prize. In *Peter Rabbit,* a mischievous rabbit embarks on an adventure unlike Archie's in motivation. He's looking for adventure, period. While Archie is surrounded by kind adults who give his pet germ in a jar a prize, Peter Rabbit feels surrounded by the antagonistic Mr. McGregor. Both characters are motivated: Archie toward achievement, Peter toward excitement.

Wrapping It Up

Motivations often do not become clear until the close of a picture book story. The ending of a picture book is a difficult technical task, requiring the balancing of satisfaction and surprise. In Gerald Rose's *The Tiger Skin Rug,* a flea-bitten tiger wanders from the jungle into a Rajah's palace, where he poses as a rug. As he enjoys the easy life, he becomes fatter and sleeker, and begins to arouse the suspicions of the household. Just when the reader is growing frantic that this beguiling tiger is going to be discovered and punished, a robber appears, and the tiger springs to life—to the relief of the household and the reader. The tiger's motivation for escaping into the comfortable palace was his inability to compete with the fierce animals of the jungle. His own animal strength wins him a permanent place in the Rajah's household. This story brings satisfaction through surprise, and part of its charm is that Rose keeps the reader on edge until the very end.

Not all picture books have such thrilling conclusions. A spectacular action at the end of a story often works very well, but some picture books have a quieter rhythm. *Where the Wild Things Are,* Maurice Sendak's story about Max and his visit to the monsters when he is angry at his mother, doesn't end until the very last word. Returning from his fantastic trip, Max is offered dinner by his mother: *And it was still hot.* This quiet conclusion after the wild unleashing of the "beast within" ties the story together perfectly, paralleling the conventional "and they lived happily ever after" wrap-up. The effect is the same, but the original, oblique way Sendak finds to express this assurance that things are back to normal makes the story satisfying in a surprising way.

Presenting the Facts

The structure of the storybook is different from that of a nonfiction picture book. The storybook depends on a variety of rhythms, or ebb and flow, whereas the informational picture book needs a steady beat with some syncopation. Many nonfiction writers for very young children find that using an obvious idea to unify their presentation of information is most effective. The classic *ABC of Cars and Trucks* is not the only children's book about cars and trucks, but its straightforward route through the alphabet gives the young reader a definite framework in which to experience all this new information. John Reiss's *Colors* starts with the primary colors, moves on to the secondary colors, and proceeds through unusual color combinations in a logical way, without any surprises. Edward Koren's inspired *Behind the Wheel,* a study of various kinds of transport as they appear to their operators, offers original combinations of technically accurate vehicles and funny furry creatures driving them, but his overall structure is straightforward.

The difference in the demands made on the young reader by storybooks and by informational picture books is evident. A child reading for information is using and developing his skill in logic, whereas a child reading for entertainment is developing his imagination. A young child's logic is a fragile thing, strengthened by constant exposure to orderly thinking. His imaginative powers are unfettered, but here too he looks for experience in exercising and stretching these powers in books. The two approaches are very different. This is one of the reasons that the hybrid informational-fictional story so often fails. Children reading for information want information; children reading for entertainment want exhilaration and relaxation.

If you are tempted to combine fiction and information, be careful not to attempt this alliance through a storybook structure packed with facts. Suppose you want to acquaint a child with the importance of caring for his teeth. (I offer teeth as an example because dental hygiene is a popular subject with writers for the picture book age—any children's book editor sees at least ten teeth manuscripts a year.) You have several choices:

1. You can personify the child's teeth as friendly little creatures who want to help in combatting the monster Donald Decay.
2. You can contrast the stories of Harry Hygiene and Carl Cavity, showing how Harry, who takes care of his teeth, is smarter and better off than Carl, who stubbornly refuses to brush.
3. You can explain how teeth grow and decay, telling why dogs don't need to brush their teeth, for instance, but children do.
4. You can show in detail how a child cares for his teeth, letting the book be a reassuring example of the right way to have healthy teeth.

The first two examples show a calamitous confusion of fiction and nonfiction techniques. In an attempt to make the subject more accessible to the child, the techniques of fiction are introduced into what is really a nonfiction subject and the result is a bad case of the cutesies. Besides, children can tell when they are being fed a sugar-coated pill, and they consider it a betrayal. An allegorical presentation of the travels of Sam the Spermatozoon, which believe it or not I was once offered by a well-meaning but ill-advised author, just doesn't come across.

A straightforward nonfiction presentation of subjects like this works because children of the picture-book age really have quite an appetite for factual material. They have, for instance, made Aliki's *Let's Read and Find Out about Teeth* and Harlow Rockwell's *My Dentist*, which follow the outlines described in 3 and 4 above, perennial favorites.

One of the most charming books for children I've ever worked on is *What to Do When There's No One But You.* This book started out as Harriet Gore's brainstorm: telling very young children how to deal with emergencies. What to do when you cut your finger, how to act when too much sun spoils a day at the beach, how to react until an adult arrives when a child has been bitten by a snake. As a nurse and mother, Gore knew the subject and the audience well. She understood the importance of bringing the situations to life by having strong characters enacting the scenes. Her first draft included two five-year-olds, Freddy and Freda First Aid. The instinct was right, but the characters fell flat, because they weren't really childlike. What five-year-old knows what to do in a medical emergency? And it seemed equally unlikely that two children would experience every possible variation of childhood mishap.

Gore's solution was to introduce a large cast of children, each of whom appeared in the stories as a victim and a fix-it hero, so that the text was accessible to children through identification. Her solution was ambitious because the book became an interwoven series of separate stories, combining nonfiction organization with a fictional flow. Good nonfiction for the picture book age requires ingenious and hard-to-execute plotting devices like this one—and Gore's royalty statements are a testament to how worthwhile the extra effort is.

If you want to present nonfiction in a fictional format, remember that *the story comes first*. After you have developed a plot that works as it should in any story, you can enrich its educational content with accurate details of setting, authentic language, period details, and appropriate characterization. Remember that structure and plotting alone do not make a storybook. Spontaneous action, logical motivation, and believable relationships between characters are what make a storybook a story.

Children are discerning, and they resent being misled as much as they enjoy being surprised. While basic emotional conflicts, simple battles of good against evil, and homely characterizations can be enough for a picture book, children are as demanding as any adult in their expectations for consistency, motivations and consequences, and authenticity. The tight demands of the picture book plot leave the writer no room for false starts, muddled middles, and inconclusive endings. But if you frame your words in a structure that's appropriate, the conventions of picture book plotting will make your work all the easier.

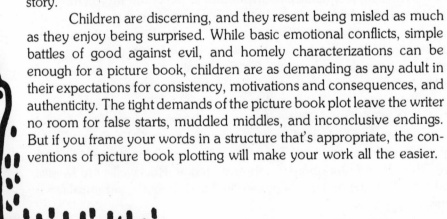

6

Picture Book Places

Once upon a time in Spain..."

So opens Munro Leaf's classic *The Story of Ferdinand* (Illustration 6-1). Even before the writer tells you who the story is about, he takes the time to tell you *where* the story takes place. The when is left vague, but the where is pinpointed. That's because the picture book is a visual medium. Setting the story in a specific spot is one approach to writing picture books that has sparked some humdingers.

All writers communicate with their readers through sensory images, but for no one is this so true as for the picture book author. The words you choose will evoke responses from all five of your readers' rapidly developing senses, especially their sight. Little kids are all eyes and ears, as any teacher can tell you, and they want stories that help them see new places and hear new sounds.

Some people are extra sharply tuned into the sounds they hear, while others miss no small detail of what they see in the world around them. By the same token, some writers naturally appeal first to the ears of young children, with memorable refrains, catchy rhymes, and natural-sounding conversations. Others make their pitch first and foremost to their readers' eyes by evoking a powerful sense of place, an awareness of the minutiae in their surroundings; by a sharpening of the looking reflex. The picture book setting is important to both these kinds of writers; the difference is in proportion only.

A story that starts with a characterization concept or a plot twist needs a setting just as a picture needs a frame, or a mousse needs a mold. In *Humbug Rabbit,* Lorna Balian introduces her leading characters in terms of their homes:

> This is Granny and the house she lives in.
> This is Father and Mother Rabbit and the burrow they live in.

Although *Humbug Rabbit*—from its title onward—is a story on an Easter theme about some memorable characters, the writer still considers the setting.

Once upon a time in Spain

Illustration 6-1.
A distinctively Spanish landscape gets The Story of Ferdinand *off to a smashing start, with Robert Lawson's dramatic rendering completing Munro Leaf's on-the-mark text.*

The half-sentences describing their habitat tell us many things about the granny and the rabbits who will star in Balian's story. As the story unfolds, where and how the rabbits and the granny live become essential to the Easter-egg hunt that is central to the action. Whether a writer is starting with a mise-en-scène or not, the story that is set in a specific spot captures the reader's interest quickly.

Many writers find that they are inspired by a setting. They may actually start with the setting and build a plot in it and around it. Their choice of characters can depend on the locale they have in mind. A character in a book with a strong setting can either fit in perfectly, like the Petrini mice family in Don Freeman's *Pet of the Met,* or they can be blatant intruders, like "the man in the yellow hat" in *Curious George.*

Caldecott Medalist Peter Spier, the author and illustrator of *The Fox Went Off on a Chilly Night, London Bridge Is Falling Down,* and *People,* is very much a places person. In *The Erie Canal,* he presents four illustrations on a double-page spread, showing the four seasons of the year on the canal to accompany the rhythmic words of the familiar folk song: *And ev'ry inch of the way we know/From Albany to Buffalo* (Illustration 6-2). He captures the sense of places in illustrations that are populated with characters who belong in the settings and that communicate this sense of place to his reader.

Glen Dines, the author and illustrator of twenty books for children, describes the reactions of the seeing writer. "When the plot calls for mood or a specific location, I find myself picturing that scene in my mind's eye. This may not be unique, except that the characters and the plot seem to develop from a visual concept or a kind of 'mental image' trigger, rather than from a word orientation."

Suppose that you want to start your picture book off with a setting. It could be the place you grew up, as it was for Maurice Sendak in *The Sign on Rosie's Door;* it could be a countryside you have visited and loved, as it was for Robert McCloskey in *Blueberries for Sal;* or it could be a place you have visited that you want to share with others, as it was for photographer David Mangurian when he created *Lito, the Shoeshine Boy,* an autobiographical essay by Lito Chirinos, a young South American. Whatever the nature of your exposure, personal familiarity is the key to evoking a powerful picture book place.

Starting off with a place immediately poses another problem. Are you introducing a place in a nonfiction vein, as Aliki does in *My Visit to the Dinosaurs* with a look at the Museum of Natural History in New York? Or do you want to create a storybook with a strong sense of place, as Ludwig Bemelmans does in *Madeline* with Paris, or as Ed and Barbara Emberley do in *The Story of Paul Bunyan* with the North Country?

And ev'ry inch of the way we know

Illustration 6-2.

A single two-page spread conveys the changes of the seasons on the Erie Canal in Peter Spier's rendering of that simple and perennially popular folk song in his book The Erie Canal.

The informational book is more objective, more tightly organized, and its illustrations are accurate if not absolutely realistic. Photographs are often featured in nonfiction treatments of picture books on a "places" theme. M. Sasek's quirky drawings and spontaneous texts in the *This Is . . .* books, including *This Is San Francisco, This Is London, This Is New York,* are full of magpie information. Instead of trying to tell the reader everything, he shares his own perception of places, describing cities and countries through his own eyes. It is as though he has offered the reader special Sasek glasses, which will show the child the world in a new way.

The storybook fixed in a given place or setting presents a complex problem, because a storybook must include very strong characters

From Albany to Buffalo.

and a plot that shows them motivated to action and dealing with the consequences of that action. It takes an enterprising author to find a way to establish a setting without shortchanging plot or characterization. Choosing a familiar setting is one way to achieve a nice balance of setting, plot, and characterization. Shirley Hughes's *George the Baby-sitter,* in which a long-haired teenager tends three small children while Mother goes to work, has a setting that is as strong as the characters. The setting, brought to life in Hughes's naturalistic full-color paintings, is a modern household. There are towels on the bathroom floor, dirty dishes on the table, broken toys on the shelves. Because the setting is so familiar to the child of a working mother, it does not make undue demands on the reader's attention. Its familiarity and authenticity mean that the writer doesn't need to waste any words describing it, and can concentrate instead on the foibles of small children "helping" the babysitter prepare for Mother's return.

James Marshall's *George and Martha* uses this familiarity in a different, but equally effective, way. George and Martha live in a house with a yard: it could be anywhere. The simple and sturdy furnishings depicted by the artist-writer are appropriate to hippos living as humans. In a similar way, in Russell Hoban's *Frances* stories (the first illustrated by Garth Williams, and the later stories by Lillian Hoban), the comfortable furniture shows that Frances's badger parents are providing a safe haven for this spirited little girl badger as she struggles with the problems of growing up—the arrival of a new baby, the celebration of her sister's birthday, the betrayal by her best friend.

A more sensational use of setting is featured in storybooks about regional heroes, such as *The Story of Paul Bunyan*. Here the terrain—the North Woods—motivates the character's actions. It is a larger-than-life setting, and Paul Bunyan thrives in it, as he could not thrive in a classroom or in a suburban neighborhood. In *Pop Corn and Ma Goodness*, Edna Mitchell Preston writes of the universal cycles of life and death, merriment and sadness that characterize family history. The Ozark setting dictates actions that are peculiar to the setting—Pop Corn kills a b'ar, for instance—but with another setting the same qualities could be shown in different ways.

In Don Freeman's *Pet of the Met*, the venerable Metropolitan Opera House in New York City is the star of the story (Illustration 6-3). The reader gets a definite idea of onstage and backstage, the prompter's box, the orchestra pit, the attic, and the vast, dazzling auditorium through the Petrini family's eyes. Freeman contrasts the cozy existence of the mouse family with the excitement of the grand old building.

The jungle is as important to *The Story of Babar* as the opera house is to *Pet of the Met*. But in this case, the setting distances the story. In Freeman's tale the setting is brought close to the reader. But in *The Story of Babar* the faraway quality of the setting enables the author to address big emotional concerns of the reader without being downright frightening. Early in the story of Babar, the little elephant sheds tears over his dead mother, who a page before had been rocking him gently in his hammock. This is a sad, sad picture. It is tolerable, however, because de Brunhoff has used an exotic setting to distance the horrible event of Babar's mother's death. Imagine if the setting were a suburban house with a yard with an Anchor fence and a car in the driveway. In a familiar locale, the death of the hero's mother would inspire nightmares in the young reader, and he would slam the book shut without ever turning the pages to find out what happened next.

In *Curious George*, Hans Rey uses this distancing device in a different way. He moves from the remote jungle where mischief has life-

Illustration 6-3.
In Pet of the Met *the old Metropolitan Opera House is the setting for Don Freeman's family of mice, the Petrinis, here perched under the railing for their favorite opera,* The Magic Flute.

and-death consequences for a little monkey to a modern city where a child can experience mild punishment for mischief instead of harm. George, a "naughty little monkey," lives in the jungle, which we know is full of fierce lions, tigers, and elephants. Trusting others so much that he lets curiosity outweigh caution, George is captured—or should I say saved—by "the man in the yellow hat." This nice man takes George to a place where he can indulge his curiosity without getting hurt: there are no tigers, lions, or elephants in the America where George moves. He gets into trouble, but he doesn't get hurt. When he is punished, he is punished in a loving, teaching way. Rey moves his story from the threatening world of the jungle to the reassuring world of a modern American city which children recognize and enjoy.

The distancing device in picture book settings works very well for "scary" stories. Problems arise, however, when the writer uses the distancing device for unscary, maybe even dull, stories. An exotic setting cannot save a story that has no intrinsic interest, no life. Too many authors try to write about their vacation trips here and there without taking the time to research and experience the exotic spot. It is as if they said, "Oh, let's take this trip as a tax deduction," without considering how it would make a book that would excite readers.

Travel as Research

Involvement is an essential ingredient in picture book writing. Some people have a natural propensity for involvement with places, and a fortnight in France, or China, or Vermont can give them enough to work from to make a very satisfactory book. Most people, though, need more exposure than a two-week stint can offer in order to absorb the impact of a place. If you would like to use a trip you are taking as the basis for a picture book, do some homework first. Go to the library, the travel agency, the tourist office, and read everything you can find about your destination. Keep a journal about the places you want to visit, and record your expectations. This preliminary searching for the sense of the place will open your eyes once you get there to aspects of the locale that the unprepared tourist would never discover.

Mariana Prieto, the author of *The Fleas of the Panther,* Cuban by birth and American by adoption, finds that travel in Spanish-speaking countries revives her early memories, her childhood sense of the magic of a place, and that this is essential to her writing. Anne Rose, who adapts folktales and traditional stories to the picture book form, travels to the places where her stories originated to reinforce her command of the details. For her funny *How Does a Czar Eat Potatoes?* Rose traveled to the Soviet Union to do research. Her immersion in the country, its customs, its culture, and its characters gives this simple tale a solid confidence that is reassuring and enduring.

Once you start your trip, make it a point to buy postcards first thing. Study the cards, and as you take your own pictures, take care not to duplicate the scenes you already have. Make an extra effort to see the place through your own eyes, to capture the aspects of the locale and its people as *you* see them. Don't be such an industrious researcher that you don't allow yourself some reflective moments, though, to discover how you feel about the place, what you like and don't like, what is really exotic and what is just a variation of what you already know.

You will discover that some places make better settings than others. And you may find that it's people, not places, that influence you more. You may start out a trip thinking that the setting is going to be inspiration for your new book, and discover that it's an old man you meet on a train whose personality sets off a great idea for a children's book.

On the other hand, many writers start off with a snippet of conversation, an amusing observation, or a feisty character, but discover that their book only comes together when they set it in a certain spot. For these writers, the setting is not especially important in the idea stage, but that doesn't mean that the setting can't change what they had conceptualized before they'd put their story in a place. A setting can enrich a characterization or a plot. When Linda Glovach wrote *The Cat and the Collector,* she first focused on her character, an old man who made his living by scavenging from the garbage, and lived with his faithful cat. When he befriends a little bird, the cat becomes jealous, and, exercising his instincts, kills the bird. The character of the collector is strong and believable, the plot compelling and exciting. But the real mood of the book is set up by the small town where the collector lives. As the collector seeks the cat whom he has banished for killing his beloved bird, the reader gets a sense of the hills and streets and weather in a small town. The setting was not Glovach's inspiration for the story or the motivation for writing it, but it emerges as strongly as the plot and characterization.

The setting can be an adjunct to a picture book or the inspiration for it, but either way, its importance cannot be underestimated. Because a picture book is a seeing experience, the sense of place is paramount. How you handle the setting depends on your outlook and personality, but awareness of the setting as an essential component of your story will help you to swiftly bring your reader the answer to the question "where?"

7

Picture Book Principles

In a picture book, setting, plot, and characterization are conveyed in words and sentences, not paragraphs and chapters. Some writers find this length limitation a trial; others consider it a challenge, a showcase for their skill with language. Length is not the only limitation, of course, but it *is* the essential one. Concise writing is a special discipline for the author, and a special treat for the reader. It's fun to read a closely worded advertisement, a meticulously wrought poem, a crisply reported newspaper article. In between times, though, adult readers can turn to leisurely novels, long, complex histories, or fascinating, rambling memoirs. For the child, concise writing is a steady diet. The storybook is the child's novel, the concept book his philosophical treatise, and informational books his history or science books. He welcomes poetry, jokes, riddles, and folktales, too, but his most insistent demand is for the illusion of escape into *literature,* a literature with a minimum of words, but words that are just difficult enough to stretch the child's imagination and reading ability. In describing "a splendid use of language," novelist Shirley Hazzard speaks of "single words forming entire narrations, phrases deployed like color in a painting." This is the picture book writer's goal.

Between the ages of two and four, when a child is making his first acquaintance with books, his use of words is changing from a naming game, in which his vocabulary is over 50 percent simple nouns, to some more ambitious combinations. By the end of his fourth year, the child's vocabulary is only 20 percent nouns, with increasing numbers of verbs, adjectives, and adverbs enriching his ability to understand and communicate through words. Although many outstanding writers for children fight the idea of a controlled text, which they say can't possibly stretch a child's imagination or ability, it would be absurd to expect a full-scale novel or long narrative poem to hold a child's attention as effectively as the hijinks of Sendak's Rosie in *The Sign on Rosie's Door.*

Lists exist of the few hundred words that children in the first grade have learned to say and read and even spell, but they are beside the point. Your book can include the thousands and thousands of words in our vocabulary-rich language, which these same children can decipher, say, understand, and master—with delight—from the printed page. Since picture books are shared by children with adults, the controls on vocabulary are not as important in them as they are in the first independent reading books children encounter between the ages of six and nine. (Dr. Seuss's *Cat in the Hat* is one such "easy reader.") For the picture book age, the author is safe in introducing words children hear in conversation but have never had a chance to see in print. The picture book reader has not yet mastered complex language, but an occasional big word—spectacular! thingamajig!—enhances his awareness of the intricacies of language and reinforces his command of the words he hears.

In *Stone Soup,* Marcia Brown describes men returning from war: "Three soldiers trudged down the road in a strange country." In *The Story of Ferdinand,* Munro Leaf introduces exotic terms when the "fierce" Ferdinand refuses to fight: "And the Banderilleros were mad and the Picadores were madder and the Matador was so mad he cried because he couldn't show off with his cape and sword." And in *The Tale of Benjamin Bunny,* Old Mrs. Rabbit cries, "Cotton-tail! Cotton-tail! fetch some more camomile." All of these authors could have taken refuge in the safe territory of controlled vocabulary, but each chose instead to use colorful words that convey precise images—*trudging* soldiers, mad *Banderilleros, camomile.* Not a child in a hundred will know what camomile is, but all adore the alliteration.

For the child just learning language, even simple words like *bear* or *orange* or *yelled* have an excitement many adults have forgotten how to comprehend.

The writer who wants to reach very young children, the two- to four-year-olds, will exploit their love of naming objects, recognizing them, studying the environment of each object, as in the conventional initiation into reading, the alphabet book. Fritz Eichenberg's *Ape in a Cape* offers a simple rhyming phrase about an animal for each letter, but he would drive a strict reading teacher up the wall with his playing with words, as in "H: hare at the fair." Yet it's this very playfulness that enables adults to read the book over and over to children without being bored to tears. It also introduces children to the idea of homophones before they study them systematically—in short, it makes learning reading easier and more fun by taking a bit of poetic license rather than following primer rules.

The picture book is *not* a textbook: it is a reading-for-fun book, usually experienced before a child starts his formal reading and writing education. Thoughtful teachers turn to picture books to inspire and mo-

Illustration 7-1.

The peddler who loses his temper in Esphyr Slobodkina's Caps for Sale *receives an onomatopoetic reception ("Tsz, tsz, tsz.") from the monkeys he meets. The re-creation of animal sounds is a favorite device in books to be read aloud.*

tivate children to learn the lessons the reading primer or spelling book teaches; thoughtful parents share books with children long before school starts in order to whet the appetite for language. Thus, even in the very beginning books—the counting books, the alphabet books, the "awareness" books, which address such childhood concerns as Mommy's pocketbook and nighttime noises—the picture book author has poetic license. It's his exploitation of this poetic license that will make or break the text.

Poetic principles are a picture book writer's basic tools. Metaphor, that essential ingredient of all poetry, is indispensable to the picture book writer, in choice of language as much as in choice of subject.

Since animals are so widely used as picture book characters, the onomatopoetic verbs of sound—roar, whine, hum, buzz, growl, bark—all have special value in picture book writing (Illustration 7-1). Animal characters serve a dual purpose, introducing the child to the creatures that surround him as well as standing in for humans as universal personalities. The first of these purposes has less immediacy than it did a couple of generations ago; most young children now know dogs and cats and goldfish and gerbils as pets, and have little exposure to the beasts of the farm and the forest that were their grandparents' constant companions. But the second, metaphorical purpose holds true—we know naughty little girls who are as clever and funny as monkeys, toddlers who tumble about like puppies; then there's the homely gray-

Illustration 7-2.
Marie Hall Ets creates a lush forest in black and white in her book In the Forest. *In this charming illustration the little boy with his new horn and paper hat encounters a napping lion.*

haired babysitter who unsettlingly resembles a wolf, or a pudgy neighbor who has a pig's round cheeks and awkward gait.

In Marie Hall Ets's *In the Forest,* a little boy's fantasy plays on animal images: for instance, the lion with the unkempt mane (Illustration 7-2):

> I had a new horn and a paper hat
> And I went for a walk in the forest.
> A big wild lion was taking a nap
> But he woke up when he heard my horn.
> "Where are you going?" he said to me.
> "May I go too if I comb my hair?"

Feodor Rojankovsky describes his own initiation into children's book illustration, inspired by a trip to the zoo at an early age: "Two great events determined the course of my childhood. I was taken to the zoo and saw the most marvelous creatures on earth and while my admiration was running high, I was given a set of crayons." As long as there are zoos and pets and national parks and lakes and forests, animal metaphors will be alive and well.

People can be metaphorical too. *The Five Chinese Brothers* is a classic children's book which has fallen out of favor because of its apparent stereotypical depiction of five Chinese brothers who look exactly alike. In it the author, Claire Huchet Bishop, describes how a boy's life is saved by the abilities of his brothers, each of whom can perform one astonishing, superhuman feat—withstanding terrific heat; drinking the ocean dry. This is not an informational book about China, or a heroic tale about strength in the face of the forces of evil—it is simply a hilarious exploration of the functions of the human body. The child perceives the universe largely in relation to his body, and Bishop's imaginative and comical tale dramatizes the universal but near-indescribable experience of simply having a body.

Verse—or Doggerel?

Rhyme is one of the most effective (and most misused) forms of picture book writing. Many publishers will not even consider rhyming manuscripts, so abysmally low, so singsong, is the overall level of the verse. Yet when rhyme is skillfully handled in a picture book, it triumphs. In *Madeline* (Illustration 7-3), Bemelmans's telling choice of detail couched in lively, unmonotonous verse sets off his richly detailed pictures of a convent school in early-twentieth-century Paris:

> In an old house in Paris that was covered with vines,
> Lived twelve little girls in two straight lines.

Everybody had to cry—

not a single eye was dry.

Madeline was in his arm

in a blanket safe and warm.

Illustration 7-3.

Rhyming couplets and spot illustrations enliven the pace in the classic Madeline, *by Ludwig Bemelmans. Here the single-sentence rhymes speak volumes as the exciting story progresses.*

> In two straight lines they broke their bread,
> And brushed their teeth,
> And went to bed.

In *Pop Corn and Ma Goodness,* Edna Mitchell Preston uses rhyme and the principles of meter to enrich a simple chronicle of a family's struggle through life, love, death, and birth. Her word choice shows an awareness of *assonance* and *alliteration*.

> Ma Goodness she's coming a-skippitty skoppetty
> skippitty skoppetty
> skippitty skoppetty
> Ma Goodness she's coming a-skippitty skoppetty
> All doon the hill.

Probably the most famous rhymer of all is Dr. Seuss. An index of his popularity is the number of imitators he has. The apparent ease of his verse and his madcap nonsense have inspired so many untalented poets to mimic him that editors cringe when they see a manuscript trumpeting the author as the "new" Dr. Seuss. What Dr. Seuss achieves through rhyme is humor, simplicity, and zany unexpected twists.

In *The Five Hundred Hats of Bartholomew Cubbins,* he blends rhyme and nonsense to create a sense of magic as the king's magicians chant over Bartholomew:

> "Winkibus
> Tinkibus
> Fotichee
> Klay,
> Hat on this demon's head,
> Fly far away!
> Howl, men, howl away,
> Howl away, howl away,
> Yowl, cats, yowl away,
> Yowl away, yowl away!
> Hat on this demon's head,
> Seep away, creep away, leap away, gleap away,
> Never come back!"

Many parents are eager to have their children master quickly as much reading vocabulary as possible. Rhyme offers a painless and often pleasant repetition of similar sounds, so that simply by identifying the initial consonants the child is able to build both his vocabulary and his confidence.

The writer who wants to create picture books in rhyme has to bear in mind that a basic structure of rhyming words is just as important as the surprise that an occasional deviation can create. Barbara Shook Hazen understands this; in *Where Do Bears Sleep?* she creates a solid rhyming structure *before* she brings in a delicious surprise twist:

> Birds rest in nests.
> Some nest in a tree.
> Some nest in cliffs overlooking the sea.
> Some in sedges, some in hedges,
> and some on ledges
> Precariously.

For all the appeal of apparent spontaneity in the poetry for a picture book, rhyming text has to be more carefully wrought than prose exposition. Because the words roll off the tongue so easily and often hilariously, the author is tempted to substitute silliness for sense. And without good sense—even in nonsense—the picture book does not cohere.

Repetition, the heart of music, poetry, and song, builds a structure as sturdy as rhyme. In *May I Stay?* Harry Allard uses repetition to tell the story of an old and weary traveler who asks at a country house, "May I stay?" In reply, each character repeats, "I am not the boss, you must ask my father," until, nine interviews later, a wizened old man replies, "Yes, you may stay." This picture-book retelling of an old Norse legend telescopes a long time span into a single short story through repetition.

Tricks with language needn't be complex to be effective. In *Andy and the Lion,* James Daugherty ends each of a key sequence of pages of his cliff-hanger tale with the beginning of the next.

At last they both stopped for breath. The lion held out his paw to show Andy what was the matter. It was a big thorn stuck in his paw. But (page turn)

Andy had an idea. He told the lion to just be patient and they'd have that thorn out in no time. Fortunately (page turn)

Andy always carried his pliers in the back pocket of his overalls. He took them out and got a tight grip. Then (page turn)

And so on, until Andy pulls the thorn out—and meanwhile the reader is left breathless to turn each page!

Remy Charlip takes a similar virtuosity with adverbs one step further in *Fortunately.*

Unfortunately he ran into a deep dark cave.
Fortunately he could dig.

The culmination of a series of unfortunate circumstances alternating with fortunate ones is a birthday party.

In *Pierre,* one of the four titles in *Nutshell Library,* Maurice Sendak uses the refrain "I don't care" at irregular intervals throughout to unify his story of a little boy whose response to every parental comment is "I don't care." When Pierre's parents depart and he is left with a lion who threatens to eat him, his response is still the same. After his parents rescue him, though, the refrain changes to suit the happy ending: riding on the lion's back with his parents, Pierre shouts, "Yes, indeed, I care!"

I have laid a great deal of stress, and rightly, on the importance of simplicity in a picture book; but elegance and authenticity must never be sacrificed for mere brevity, in the name of simplicity. It is easy enough to telescope a paragraph into a sentence by forgoing adjectives and adverbs and cramming that single sentence with subordinate clauses, but that kind of sloppy shortcut is not your aim. What you do want is to achieve mood and magic with carefully chosen detail and language.

Think about *every* word you use. Can you use *sobbed* instead of *cried* to good advantage? Do you want to squander your allowance of words on a reminder that your hero has blond hair, or should you count on the pictures for that? Will the use of rhyme or assonance impart a desirable rhythm to your text? These are decisions that only you can make, word by word, sentence by sentence.

> Next morning when the manager came to open the door of the laundromat, there was Lisa waiting.
>
> "I left something here yesterday," she explained. "May I look around?"
>
> "Certainly," said the manager. "My customers are always leaving things."

In this ordinary exchange from *A Pocket for Corduroy,* Don Freeman sets up the whole situation: Lisa's anxiety about her lost teddy bear Corduroy, the manager's kindliness, the reassuring commonplaceness of Lisa's mistake in leaving something important behind. Freeman uses no particular literary devices or tricks to achieve his end—he simply uses direct language to launch his plot and characterization.

A sharp eye and a keen ear are indispensable to a writer for the picture book age, and on-the-mark observation has to be communicated through meticulous choice of words and exacting sentence construction. Conciseness, excitement, and unity are your aims; so don't confuse directness with density, or simplicity with slickness. There is a world of difference, and children are very sensitive to that difference.

A Plan for Writing

There are as many different ways to write a picture book as there are to build a house. The plan I am setting forth in this chapter is just one way, but like any design, it can be adapted to suit your needs and aspirations, your strengths and limitations.

A basic principle of getting your picture book down on paper is to balance spontaneity with organization. Achieving this balance is the most difficult exercise this side of tightrope walking, as any picture book author can tell you—and it is crucial. Spontaneity, as you will see for yourself, requires a surprising amount of discipline. Organizing ideas takes discipline, too, of course, yet organization is a task many writers find relaxing, much as arranging flowers or mowing the lawn can be. This is because only serious writers are aware of how demanding and involving the seemingly passive experience of inspiration can be. Like a baseball game or a ballet, the process of writing draws simultaneously on the writer's creativity and his technical skill. To meet both these requirements, you will need a clear mind, some private, quiet time, and strong motivation to keep your ideas flowing as you write them down.

The first common, and serious, mistake a picture book writer can make is to skimp on materials—and his materials are *ideas*. Pencils and paper and elbow grease are vital, too, but ideas are essential. Just as a great architect searches for just the right wood or glass, so you must be willing to search far and wide to collect an array of ideas to write about. You won't use every idea you find, but the larger the pool from which you can choose, the better you can create the story you have in mind.

Professional picture book writers have various ways of gathering ideas. Edna Miller, the author of many picture books about a white-footed mouse called Mousekin, finds that her collecting of book ideas is essentially an exercise in observation: "Nature writes her own stories," she says. "The writer simply takes the time to watch and write them down." At the other end of the spectrum is award-winning author-illustrator Tomie de Paola, who deliberately searches out stories from many different sources, and in writing finds a voice appropriate to the mood of each subject. He studies folktales and legends from all over the world, he considers very carefully the questions asked by children he meets, and he gleans anecdotes from his own childhood and his family history. "I am open to any new idea, because the most unpromising beginnings can become, with time and thought, wonderful books." The range of his work, which includes *Our Lady of Guadaloupe,* a serious religious story, *Andy: That's My Name,* a concept book introducing the letters of the alphabet, and *The Songs of Fog Maiden,* a beautiful and personal poem, shows how effective this eclectic approach can be.

Different as their approaches are, these two writers gather ideas with a discipline that might seem startlingly methodical, even ponderous, to a nonprofessional. But they understand, after working with many good editors in the children's book field over decades, that the author initially is his own best editor. And an editor is only as good as the material he has to work with. "Writing is one of those things held closely to you, and is as personal as the color of your eyes and hair," Francine Jacobs Alberts says about her nature writing for children.

The Bright-Ideas Journal

A journal, one of the most personal forms of writing, is a good starting point for any writer. Its role is even more important for the children's picture book writer than it is for a novelist, because the picture book writer must express his ideas in a concise, refined form. As poet Richard Armour notes in his characteristically ironic way, "Most likely a novelist has to have only one idea every three or four years. I must have a new idea a little oftener than one every other day, seven days a week—or three-quarters of an idea a day."

In your journal, your thoughts, flashes of insight, and surges of inspiration are recorded. Since the journal may become your basic source of information for writing, you will want to start by choosing a notebook that has a direct appeal and usefulness for you. Make a special expedition to buy a bound blank book, and choose it with the care you would use in choosing a kitten or a puppy, because it will be your companion for a long time. It should be thick enough—at least a hundred pages—to hold a meaningful record of your ideas and inspiration over a period of months. Keep it in a special place—and keep it to yourself.

James Trivers, the author of *The Red Fire Book,* doesn't breathe a word about his ideas, his approach, or the lovable characters he's invented until the final manuscript is letter-perfect. "It's tempting to talk about new projects at a cocktail party," Trivers admits, "but talking takes energy away from writing. My rule is 'Don't tell, show,' and you can't show until the characters have their costumes, the stage is set, and the plot reveals the characters fully."

With the passion a teenage girl brings to her secret diary, you can train yourself to write down your ideas in your journal every day, even when you think you're uninspired or just too busy. Are you really busy, or are you falling into the Next Week's Chores Syndrome, indulging in busywork to avoid the harder work of creation? If you have no special thoughts for the day, seek out some stimulation—walk in the woods, strike up a conversation with a child, visit an art museum, browse through the children's book section of your library. Bernard Most's picture book *Boo!* developed from his son Eric's bedtime question, "Daddy, do monsters ever get scared of people?" Barbara Emberley, who wrote the text for the award-winning *One Wide River,* and John Langstaff, who created *Frog Went A-Courtin',* produced appealing and very different picture books from two very similar song sources. Judy Delton, the author of *It Happened on Thursday,* looks to newspaper items for inspiration. Franz Brandenberg, author of *No School Today!* and *I Wish I Was Sick, Too!,* finds that the routines of modern life, like going to school and moving, form the basis for his lighthearted and reassuring stories.

Make mental notes of the activities that stimulate you most. It could be something as seemingly unrelated to children as gardening, or something as direct as photographing children at play. Be adventurous: explore the world around you.

The secret of the bright-ideas journal is to refrain from looking back through it, at least for a time. Approaching each new day with a clean sheet, untrammeled by the moods and reactions of the day before, will give you a long view of your recurring interests, your observations on different subjects that dovetail with one another. After you have recorded a month's random notes without missing a day, set aside an evening or an afternoon, free from distractions, and look over what you have written. After you have read it through, it is time to *think*. Try to clear your mind and remember what you have written. What comes to your mind first? Why did you think of that one idea before the myriad others you wrote about? Is there anything in your journal that surprises you? Are there passages that bring tears to your eyes or a smile to your lips? Imagine as you read that the journal was kept by someone else: what kind of person does the writing itself conjure up? Is it a truthful reflection of yourself? A funny person? A people person, or a places person, or a things person?

The Bright-Ideas File

After you have spent a good long time pondering what you have written about, you are ready to begin creating a file of bright ideas. You will need a pen, a stack of 3x5 cards, and a sturdy file box. You will also need a lot of discipline and no distractions, because you will be arranging your ideas with the detachment and precision of a researcher tabulating statistics. This is a step that is particularly important to the picture book author, because each idea has to be book-sized: not too slight, not too unwieldy. For instance, your journal might include an entry like this one:

> The way Johnny sighed when Stevie threw the ball to home plate for an out gave him away. His downcast eyes, his slumped shoulders belied the forced cheer that came out of his mouth. I finally understood how hard it is for a boy to see his best friend succeed where he has failed. He was torn between pride in Stevie and shame for himself.

This observation might end up on the file card under the heading *Baseball* as "The left fielder saves the day by covering for his friend, the daydreaming center" and again under *Sportsmanship:* "Conflict between being a good sport and wanting to be a star," and perhaps again under *Friendship:* "Single sports action precipitates a crisis of loyalty vs. competition between two boys as they grow up and change side by side."

On the next page, you will see a list of possible ideas for index card entries. This is not a comprehensive list, or even a suggested one. It is simply a starting point for you to develop your own categories, based on your own interests and experiences.

In contrast to your spontaneity in jotting down observations and ideas in your journal, you will want to set up your card file with a tough professionalism. The cards should be kept in their own box, alphabetically arranged.

After you have systematically arranged the thoughts of thirty days, you will almost certainly find that you have chosen certain themes, like sports or social situations, as ones that hold day-to-day interest for you. Some people who have captured your interest may even have been growing into full-fledged picture book characters right there in your journal.

Like your journal, this box is a secret. You may be tempted to show off your many ideas to your friends, fellow writers, or teachers, but don't succumb to the temptation: The longer your ideas are kept your private property, the more forcefully they will emerge in your

SAMPLE CARD FILE ENTRIES	
Suggested Categories	**Specific Examples**
WEATHER	hurricanes rainy Saturdays blizzards lightning spring sunshine
FAMILY RELATIONSHIPS	sibling rivalry divorce new baby grandparents absent parent
LEARNING CONCEPTS	alphabet numbers sizes shapes correspondences sets
DAILY ROUTINES	getting dressed going to bed shopping chores
ETHICAL CONCEPTS	sharing competition loyalty
CHARACTERS	braggart clown spoilsport tattle tale
RECREATION	playground sports practice team play dress-up
BIOGRAPHY	cowboys magicians rock stars athletic champions

SAMPLE CARD FILE ENTRIES	
Suggested Categories	**Specific Examples**
HEALTH	nutrition grooming exercise hygiene first aid
LOCAL COLOR	haunted houses tales of bravery Indian myths pioneer tales
RESPONSIBILITY	being on time forgetting losing things manners
ANIMALS	pets wild animals zoo friends dinosaurs endangered species
FANTASY CREATURES	mythological beasts monsters extinct animals creatures of imagination
FRIENDSHIPS	making new friends friendships under siege
SOCIALIZING CONCEPTS	school spending allowance good neighbor behavior stealing lying shyness
FANTASY AND FOLKTALES	myths legends fairy tales heroes heroines gods of ancient cultures ethnic tales science fiction

---

SAMPLE CARD FILE ENTRIES

Suggested Categories	Specific Examples
TRIPS AND OUTINGS OF ALL KINDS	visiting relatives going for a walk alone a trip downtown camping
CHANGES AND TRANSFORMATIONS	eggs to birds building a bridge night and day changes of seasons growing up
MEMORIES AND FAMILY STORIES	ethnic tales immigrant stories farm anecdotes growing up long ago
SPECIAL DAYS	birthdays holidays first days religious celebrations

---

manuscript. Imagine that they are old friends: the longer the wait between visits, the happier you will be to see them. Build up anticipation in yourself, and communicate this anticipation to others. When the curtain finally rises on your finished story, people who have not sat in on the rehearsals will respond enthusiastically.

When you have finished compiling the ideas in their many forms on index cards, take a piece of masking tape and seal up the pages of your journal that you have filled. You are now ready to follow the same process for the month ahead, unfettered by your previous observations. Masking tape can be removed when you have completed the whole journal, but it will help you resist the temptation to dwell upon what you were thinking and writing earlier. We all tend to cling to ideas that have become stale, simply because they are familiar. If you allow yourself to work on ideas that captured your interest a month ago, you will find that you aren't growing. Once you have actually written a manuscript, you will want to go back and read your journal for insights you may have overlooked, but now you want freshness and enthusiasm, two qualities achieved only by letting yourself go forward without looking back. By forcing yourself to look ahead, you will discover things about yourself that perhaps you never consciously knew: that you are more interested in weather than you are in the seasons, that the friendship between the two kids down the street triggers your memories of a childhood alliance you were sure would never end, or that you have that second cup of coffee every morning because you are fascinated by the never-ending battle between the squirrel and blue jay at the bird feeder. You may create word portraits of people you never thought were that important, or evocative descriptions of places you have come to take for granted, as you scrutinize them more closely.

The card file is the beginning of your organization of ideas. Alternating spontaneity, which will give your story life, with rigor, which will give it structure, is the secret of writing, in a way that is your own, a picture book manuscript that meets professional standards.

The First Draft

After you have built up the card file over a period of three or four months, you are ready to write. By this time you should be brimming with ideas, bursting with incidents, your fingers itching to tap the typewriter keys. Peruse the card file. Close the box. Look through your journal for the past month. Put it on the shelf. Sit down at your typewriter, or pick up your pen, pull out a piece of blank paper, and let your ideas lead you along.

For many writers, this first draft is the most satisfying part of the writing process. For others, it is torture. Some writers can't get started. That's a problem, but believe it or not, not a very serious one. Close your eyes, concentrate hard, and write down one of your journal observations. Expand on it, elaborate, describe, explain it—see? It's becoming a story!

Then there is the middle-muddler. The first paragraph is a snap, the characters are well-conceived, the mood established, and you can't wait to get to the great ending you thought of last Wednesday. But how to get from the beginning to the end? The middle-muddling writer of picture books has the advantage over similarly afflicted writers of other kinds of books because the picture book has a definite structure. This is not a magic formula, but it might be a helpful model: first establish the setting, then introduce the characters; create a conflict, then resolve it; and finally return to the comfortable familiarity of the original setting. This approach to plotting is about as exciting as a prefabricated house, but it will get you through the first round.

And what if you know what you want to happen, but can't get from this sentence to that one? Resist the temptation to rip the page out of the typewriter and start over. If you are stuck and can't squeeze another pertinent word out of your head without changing the subject, re-type your previous sentence. Do it five times if you have to. Boredom is a great spur to creating a new action, introducing a new idea. If you're still stuck, rework your previous sentence three different ways: expand it into two sentences, condense it into a shorter sentence, rewrite it following the same sentence structure but substituting synonyms for every single noun, adjective, and verb. Each of these tricks will open up your mind a crack, and soon you will be breezing along again.

At some point your story will come to an end. Don't worry if you reach this point in twenty sentences or twenty pages. Say what you want to say. Many picture book writers don't even try to stick to the subject. They indulge in extraneous ideas, introduce characters who will later disappear, and describe settings in detail, even though they know the descriptions will be edited out. Because your finished manuscript is going to be so concise, so brief, in its final form, length is unimportant in the early stages. So is vocabulary. A picture book is a book to be read aloud, to be enjoyed by adults as well as children. As discussed earlier in this chapter, there are really no limitations on vocabulary in a well-written picture book. In *Blueberries for Sal,* which has been enjoyed by two- to six-year olds for thirty years, Robert McCloskey describes a bear cub discovering Sal's mother's pail of blueberries:

> Little Bear padded up and peeked into her pail. Of course, he only wanted to taste a *few* of what was inside, but there were so many and they were so close together that he tasted a Tremendous Mouthful by mistake.

"Tremendous" and "mouthful" aren't on any first-grade vocabulary list, but there's no mistaking the author's meaning.

You will be able to make the shorter manuscript longer, and you will be able to make the longer manuscript shorter, as you edit and rewrite your work. Because they are so simple, the great picture book texts *seem* to have taken no more than an hour to write, but that is an illusion. As you struggle with an eight-page manuscript that you know should be only two pages long, remember that you are in good company: Robert McCloskey and Maurice Sendak literally spend years on their picture books, including *Make Way for Ducklings* and *Outside Over There.*

⑨

Polishing Your Manuscript

No matter how long your first draft is, the acid test is its balance. Before you decide that there really isn't enough to work with—or, at the other extreme, that it really must be expanded into a novel—take a colored pen and draw a line to indicate your manuscript's halfway point. Then break each of the two sections into halves again, then quarters, then eighths. Read a random sixteenth: does it stand on its own? What is it saying? Can it be expanded, or cut? Consider each segment individually. Do not rewrite. Do not retype. Take out here, add there, to make each of the sixteen segments balance the others, so that every segment of your picture book makes a relatively equal contribution to the whole story.

Preparing a Dummy

When you are satisfied that the balance is roughly right, take a pair of scissors and actually snip your manuscript into sixteen separate pieces. Take eight sheets of 8½x11 paper (blank on both sides!) and fold them in half horizontally. Score the fold with a table knife so that the pages don't fall away. This is your dummy. Starting with the first page (which is a right-hand page), number the pages from one to thirty-two. (Go back to Chapter 1 if you want to know why I've chosen this peculiar number.)

Using rubber cement or masking tape, to give yourself the freedom to move things around later, fix the first of your sixteen segments of text on page 1, then the next on pages 2 and 3, the next 4 and 5, and so on until you reach page 31. Page 32 will be blank, because traditionally it does not contain the story proper. It is called the *tailpiece,* and you might remember from your own days of reading picture books how satisfying the final page was with its "The End" or "Good night" or simply an amusing or lovely small drawing, such as the tailpiece of *Stone Soup* (see Illustration 1-8).

After you have pasted everything into position, read your dummy as if it were a book. Does each page make you want to turn to

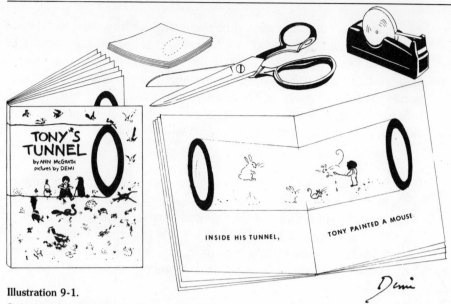

Illustration 9-1.

Scissors and scotch tape are all you need to cut and paste your dummy from a carbon of your manuscript.

the next? Does each spread of two pages lend itself to a lively and captivating visual interpretation? Is the beginning intriguing? Is the middle interesting? Is the end satisfying?

After you have studied your dummy, it's time to put it aside for a while—a day, a week, even a month. This fallow period will give you valuable distance and a fresh outlook, so that as you look over your dummy again, you will bring new insight to the exciting process of editing your own manuscript. Of the sixteen segments you have written, some are simply not going to measure up to the very best writing you can do. Some pages can be eliminated, or incorporated into other pages, or condensed. The exercise of dividing your manuscript into sixteen segments is designed to force you to eliminate at least one segment, and possibly two or three or even four. Segments can be condensed and combined at this stage, too. It is a good policy to have more text written than you can actually use in your book, because it helps you to analyze the text, weighing one passage against another, instead of accepting that first draft as perfection. Any piece of writing can be improved, and the author is the one who knows best how to improve it. At this point you are your own best editor.

As a general rule, no picture book can contain more than fifteen segments of text. There is some flexibility in how much space is left for front matter (see Chapter 1), so the author can let the writing dictate whether he should cut two spreads or four from the sixteen he has written.

As you edit out a spread or two, consider how interesting each two-page spread is. You will not be looking to match the number of words per two-page spread exactly; the important thing is to achieve a balanced interest, with each set of two pages making an equal contribution to the story as a whole. There are no formulas for this, but there are four general guidelines (each with its exceptions) that will help you decide for yourself what should stay and what should go:

1. *Each spread should contain at least one word.* It can be a simple, exciting "CRASH!" or a soothing "Good night." New readers and lap readers can find a wordless spread hard to handle. Important as pictures are, the aim of the picture book is to acquaint children with reading. Continuity is very important, and including at least a word or phrase on each spread ensures a feeling of moving along effortlessly.

2. *Each spread should have a consistent mood.* If you are evoking a thoughtful or a sad atmosphere, you will want to sustain it until the reader turns the page for the next episode. This reinforces the power of your writing in a physical way, just the right frame not only encloses a painting, but draws attention to its beauty by setting it off.

3. *Each spread should be a step.* The steps should vary in tempo, sometimes tiptoeing, occasionally leaping, most often just walking along. All the steps should be made for the same set of legs. The steps are usually steps forward, leading the reader to turn the page to see what will happen next, but at the same time, you want to begin the page with one foot firmly planted, resolving the question or consolidating the mood you have set on the previous page. In a very subtle way, the text on each spread should begin by answering a question and by asking a new one. In Ludwig Bemelmans's *Madeline,* the author writes on one page:

> In the middle of one night.
> Miss Clavel turned on the light
> and said, "Something is not right!"

and as the reader eagerly turns the page he discovers that

> Little Madeline sat in bed,
> cried and cried; her eyes were red.
> And soon after Dr. Cohn
> Came, he rushed out to the phone

By this time the reader's heart is in his throat, but he has to turn the page to discover what is going to happen next:

> and he dialed: DANton-ten-six—
> "Nurse," he said, "it's an appendix!"

The page turns enable the author to advance his plot with just a few words, because each turn of the page creates a whole new stage setting.

4. *Each spread should sustain the pace.* The task of keeping the distractable child enthralled for twelve or thirteen page turns is one of the most exacting of all writing tasks. Setting up beginnings and endings is difficult, but in picture book writing, *middles matter most.* In *Caesar, Cock of the Village,* Philippe Dumas keeps up the pace and the excitement by interspersing lushly long sentences with rhythmic short phrases on a series of two-page spreads:

> Everyone in the village went for me with whatever they could lay their hands on:
> Rastiman with his red-hot poker,
> Albert with a great long needle,
> Ma Pols with a ten-pound weight,
> Robert the baker with a two-pound loaf,

and so forth until the deliberate cadences bring the text to a fever pitch of excitement. Then the author returns to a wordier and more leisured pace as the story winds down to a satisfying close:

> Well, after that, you would have done what I did, under the circumstances, and catching sight of my good friend the seagull, up I hopped and off we flew.

Finding a rhythm suited to the story you are writing is an important part of pacing your picture book, and the dummy is the best way to determine whether your rhythm is both natural and captivating.

Dress Rehearsal

A kindergarten class listening to *Harry the Dirty Dog* is silent until the spellbinding story is over. As soon as it has ended, stories of baths and naughty pets are shouted over one another, with uninhibited enthusiasm for each child's version of the Harry story. "My brother hates baths," one child yells out. "My dog is all white and he's always dirty," another interrupts. Gene Zion has created more than an inspired story about a dog that runs away to escape his hated bath; it is a beautifully wrought tale that meets professional standards of economy, humor, and human values. This becomes clear when the book is read aloud.

Reading aloud is a very different experience from reading silently: the rhythm of the words becomes an important factor; the pacing of the story becomes dominant; and the balance of dialogue and action becomes essential to the story's progress. Wasted words engender boredom and restlessness. Your young reader is at an age where a fly buzzing or a dog barking down the block can constitute a distraction. Your job is to keep him enthralled, page after page, with words and highly refined concepts. At the same time, you are striving for a conclusion so satisfying that the child is not disappointed that the book has ended.

After you have edited your book and prepared a dummy, you are ready to read it aloud. "But it doesn't have pictures yet!" you object. This, believe it or not, is an advantage. If you can hold the interest of a group of children without showing them pictures, you know that you are well on your way to a strongly satisfying story.

Sharing your book with listeners, children and adults alike, is an essential step in writing a picture book manuscript. Some writers find that they are their own best critics, and can analyze their story's pacing and balance by reading it aloud to themselves. Other writers find workshops invaluable forums for criticism. Still others like to try their stories out on children. However you test your story's listenability, it's important to remember that ultimately the picture book is a told story with a special reading-aloud quality that needs careful cultivation.

There are many ways to read a manuscript aloud: dramatically, with a change of voice for each character; soothingly and more monotonously (in its truest sense); or punctuated with pauses for page turns and leisurely perusal of pictures (if available). Some writers find it helpful to have someone else read their story while they watch the audience. The restless adjustment of feet and legs after the story has begun suggests that the opening scene is too slow-paced. The wriggling that accompanies the complex plot turn in the middle of the story screams "Revise!" to the author. Faces still expectant after the last sentence demonstrate that the ending could be more satisfying. If your audience likes what you've written, you won't have to look for signs: you'll know.

Rules and formulas and authorial bags of tricks notwithstanding, picture book standards are not prescribed: anything is allowed as long as it works. What the writer should strive for is a story satisfying enough to make the reader feel that he has read a whole book, as complete as a meal with cake for dessert, balanced with enough excitement to grab his attention, to stimulate his interest, to surprise him.

As the picture book has evolved through trial and error, certain conventions have developed. These are conventions, mind you, not rules, but they are helpful guides for the writer who wants to simplify and even out his writing for children. As you listen to your story in private, and as you watch others listen to it at public readings, consider: (1) Does your story begin at the beginning? (2) Is the middle clear without being obvious? (3) Does the ending fall at a good stopping place?

Curtain Goes Up

Every writer who's ever thought of writing a novel has a great beginning in mind. But the greatest opening sentences are in picture books.

> Once there was a peddler who sold caps. But he was not like an ordinary peddler carrying his wares on his back. He carried them on top of his head.

or

> Once upon a time there lived a family of pigs. There was Father Pig and Mother Pig.

It's fatally easy to fudge the beginning of a picture book, easing into the story too slowly. There's simply not enough room for such indulgence. Who? What? Where? When? Why? children ask. In *Caps for Sale,* Esphyr Slobodkina plunges right into his story, following the classical model of *in medias res.* Slobodkina tickles our curiosity: what does he mean, he carried them on top of his head? What happened? Do they fall? No! Mary Rayner's beginning of *Mr. and Mrs. Pig's Evening Out* has a similar magic. Where are the children she promised us with "a family of pigs"? In this comic classic about a treacherous babysitter, Rayner sets the stage on the very first page. You may think it an extravagance to devote a whole page to the parents, but ten pages into the book, the reader wishes the parents were back again to protect their plump pink piglets from the Big-Bad-Wolf-Babysitter. Since picture books usually begin with a single right-hand page, the scene should be firmly set with adventurous words set off by a telling but unobtrusive picture. Look at your beginning again: is every word working?

The Plot Thickens

From the second page of the story on, ennui is an ever-present danger. The more adventurous your beginning, the more explaining you may have to do. This is where the great picture book maxim "Show, don't tell" comes to the writer's rescue. Action is essential: one action per double-page spread, self-contained and significant to the story. It's a tall order.

An action can be as simple as a telephone ringing, a child losing his temper, or two characters having an uncomplicated discussion. The everyday events of life at home may not seem exciting to you, but they are new and vitally interesting to the young child. "The best time of all," Leo Politi tells us in *Song of the Swallows,* "was when the old swallows taught the baby birds to fly."

Self-contained actions occur on a single page, or double-page spread, with the illustration acting as a sort of stage set for the character's conversation, thought, or activity. "Significant to the story" suggests that the action moves the story along, by telling us something about the character's motivation, by introducing a new character or element, or by having the character act on an idea of his own or someone else's. As you go through your dummy, think of each spread as a newspaper article. Is it interesting and attention-getting on its own? Do you, after having worked and lived with the manuscript so long, feel a flash of recognition that grabs your attention and a sense of anticipation that holds it? A good character promises a good beginning, a good plot promises a good ending, but only good writing can bring them together in a coherent whole.

Finale

Overeagerness to wind up the story can end it prematurely, even in the middle of the manuscript, with pages still to go. Failure to pull the threads of plot, character, and motivation together can end it too abruptly. You want to avoid both of these extremes. In the Caldecott-winning *Why Mosquitoes Buzz in People's Ears,* Verna Aardema paces the ending of her story by slowing it down before she brings it to a close.

> "Punish the mosquito! Punish the mosquito!" cried all the animals. When Mother Owl heard that, she was satisfied. She turned her head toward the east and hooted: "Hoo! Hooo! Hooooo!" And the sun came up.

Her narrative has ended, but she still waits to put on the crowning touch:

> Meanwhile the mosquito had listened to it all from a nearby bush. She crept under a curly leaf, semm, and was never found and brought before the council. But because of this, the mosquito has a guilty conscience. To this day, she goes about whining in people's ears. "Zeee! Is everyone still angry at me?" When she does this, she gets an honest answer.

The reader turns the page to see a large hand swatting a mosquito and the single word: *KPAO!*

Or, if your ending can be concluded in a single step, you might want to consider how Barbara Williams winds down *Albert's Toothache* (Illustration 9-2):

> "Well, I have just the thing to fix a toothache," said Albert's grandmother. She took her handkerchief from her purse and wrapped it around Albert's toe. Albert smiled toothlessly and got out of bed.

The ending reflects the title perfectly.

Illustration 9-2.
Albert and his understanding grandmother resolve the communication problem that is the basis for Barbara Williams' Albert's Toothache. *The touching conclusion to this hilarious story is captured in a soft pencil drawing by Kay Chorao.*

A Delicate Balance

From the beginning to the end, you will become aware of the importance of balance in your manuscript. You will want to leave room for pictures in the writing, as well as in the layout. A novelist might describe the clerk in the grocery store like this: "Mr. Grimes, a dashing walrus with a luxuriant mustache, seemed a most unlikely grocery clerk. His rimless spectacles, his gold watch chain, the elegant cut of his worn trousers all suggested that he had done something interesting, perhaps even sinister, in his early days. Yet every day, he appeared behind the register at eight-fifteen on the dot with good cheer that suggested that there was nothing in the world he would rather be doing." That same interesting walrus might be introduced this way in a picture book: "When Mother sent me to the store to buy some milk, I picked Mr. Grimes's line because he was the fastest. Usually I avoid Mr. Grimes because he gives me the creeps, but I was in a hurry to meet Gramps. A twi-night doubleheader at Comiskey Park! Even Mr. Grimes seemed slow." The picture book writer can pack a lot more action into his words because the illustrator can develop characters in the pictures, either at the writer's suggestion or at his own whim.

In adapting the story of Chanticleer from *The Canterbury Tales,* Caldecott-winner Barbara Cooney undertook a more complex balance problem. Her task was to convert Chaucer's rhymed couplets into prose that would be more accessible to youngsters unfamiliar with the story without violating the sense or flavor of the original. And as always, the balance between text and pictures had to be right, even though the text was necessarily longer than normal.

When the fox appears in the yard, the original (in Theodore Morrison's translation) reads:

> And so it happened, as he [Chanticleer] fixed his eye
> Among the herbs upon a butterfly,
> He caught sight of this fox who crouched there low.
> He felt no impulse then to strut or crow
> But cried "cucock!" and gave a fearful start
> Like one who has been frightened to the heart.

Using about the same number of words, but without the density of the original poetry, Cooney preserves the rich medieval flavor and imagery:

> Now it happened that, as he cast his eye upon a butterfly among the herbs, Chanticleer became aware of the fox lying low. He had no desire to crow then, but at once cried, "Cok! cok!" and started up like a man frightened in his heart.

Lyle remembered unhappily his days of traveling
and performing with Signor Valenti.
But in spite of everything, the two were
delighted to see each other once more.

Illustration 9-3

Bernard Waber is adventurous in varying the pace in Lyle, Lyle, Crocodile. *Here he takes the
space to explain some history as Lyle and Signor Valenti are reunited in a department store.*

Cooney's glowing, jewellike pictures, which seem to spring from the pages of an ancient breviary, are in perfect harmony with the prose.

Balancing your words against the illustrations your manuscript suggests is just one of the balances the picture book writer seeks. Balancing action and reflection is another trick. In *Thy Friend, Obadiah,* Brinton Turkle achieves such a balance:

> The bird was nowhere to be seen. "Maybe it doesn't like the snow," Obadiah told himself. "Maybe it flew away to the mainland." He was so glad it wasn't hopping along after him that he made duck tracks all the way up Jacob Slade's hill.

A third balance is that between description and action. In *Best Friends for Frances,* Russell Hoban enlivens his text with descriptions of food—which cannot be conveyed in the limited color illustrations—that are as spellbinding as the story itself:

> "That looks like a big lunch," said Frances.
> "It's nothing much," said Albert. "Four or five sandwiches and some apples and bananas and two packages of cupcakes and a quart of chocolate milk."
> "Can I wander with you?" asked Frances.
> "I only have one lunch," said Albert.

The most difficult balance of all is the pacing, from the rhythm of the story to the cadence of the words themselves as the reader moves from page to page. You need a certain uniformity to keep your story flowing, and reading the dummy aloud can give you a sense of how much should be said on each page: some actions need a lot of explaining, while others can be expressed in a simple phrase. Bernard Waber paces the complex story of *Lyle, Lyle, Crocodile* (Illustration 9-3) brilliantly. For instance, Lyle's sad stay at the zoo:

> Not wanting to seem unsociable, he decided to join the other crocodiles who were cozily piled together. Just when he thought he had gotten himself comfortable on top [page turn; new illustration], he awakened to find himself crushed to the very bottom.

The dummy allows you to look at the way you have balanced your story. Reading aloud from it gives you an awareness of the punctuation of the page turns. Like your child reader, you are using your eyes and ears. You may be surprised by the changes you make once you have pasted your manuscript into dummy form. You will find pages that made perfect sense on the continuous typed manuscript don't make much sense at all as they stand alone. You will find that descriptions that seemed almost extraneous when you wrote them now add a quiet moment to your busy story. A time will come when you stop fussing with small changes here and there. Someday you will find that you are looking at the dummy with a sense of satisfaction. It flows well. It has some great conversations, but no one could call it talky. The characters are just offbeat enough to be intriguing. That awkward spot near the end has been smoothed over.

You are ready to retype your manuscript!

Typing the final manuscript is an emotion-filled activity. As the letters and words fall on the page, you may become so enthralled with the glorious vision of them set in type that you begin to make typographical errors. The pages of expensive bond paper begin to pile up in the wastebasket. "What is *wrong* with me?" you ask yourself. "I'm a crack typist." For the same reasons mothers cry at weddings and fathers choke back tears at graduations, your pride in a job well done is mixed with a feeling of loss. This idea that struck you three years ago, the one you took to the writing workshop over a year ago because it seemed hopeless, the one that the children at the library still ask you to read, the one with the ending that just didn't seem right three short days ago—today it is finished. Suppress that urge to work it over one more time: it is finished. You'd like to crawl into the envelope with it and explain to the editor who reads it how really good it is, but you are free to go to the beach instead. Your manuscript is ready to speak for itself: it is ready to be submitted for publication.

PART THREE

A PRACTICAL GUIDE TO PUBLICATION

10

Submitting Your Manuscript

Once upon a time, when publishing was a quieter business, the aspiring author would slip his manuscript over the transom in the hopes that his work would be read. At first the "over the transom" manuscript was a rarity, indulgently read by the editor or his assistant as a reward for the writer's chutzpah. As publishing grew, and more and more writers sought to have their work published, the number of unsolicited manuscripts increased, and the junior editors assigned to read them were overwhelmed. They came to view reading these manuscripts as a dreaded task, because there simply was not enough time for them. This stack of unsolicited, and largely unwelcome, manuscripts became known as the slush pile.

In many adult departments, the slush pile is becoming obsolete. Manuscripts are returned unopened, because the crush is so great that it is no longer possible for publishers to pore over novels by unknown writers who may win the Pulitzer but haven't yet. Children's departments, however, still pay serious attention to the slush pile. Rare indeed is the editorial committee in a juvenile publishing company that does not actively seek new properties in the tidal wave of unsolicited manuscripts. Even so, while no exact figures exist for published manuscripts that started in the slush pile, I'd guess the chances are about a thousand to one. You wouldn't bet on a horse with those odds, but there are ways to improve the chances of getting your manuscript published. This chapter will concentrate on shining in the slush pile. One obvious help may be to hire an agent, and Chapter 12 explores that possibility in detail. But for the purposes of this chapter let's suppose you're submitting your manuscript "over the transom."

Remember, editors *like* to accept manuscripts. It is one of the great joys of an editor's life to discover a talent that has not been touted and hyped but speaks through the manuscript itself. So, having written a book of which you are justifiably proud, you'll naturally want to carry through that sense of pride and accomplishment in all the nonwriting aspects of submitting a manuscript.

The Package

Start with an interesting envelope. An "interesting envelope"? Publishers are book people, remember, and the whole "package," from the jacket inward, intrigues book people far more than it does John Q. Public. The "jacket" for your manuscript is the envelope in which you submit it. It doesn't have to be a screaming red, but if it is distinctive and appropriate to your style, it guarantees at least a modicum of special attention.

Any envelope's appeal is doubled if you get the editor's name right—and halved if you don't! Since children's book publishing shares the musical-chairs personnel characteristic of the publishing field as a whole, getting the editor's name right is not so easy as it might seem. *Writer's Market* lists the names and addresses of publishing houses and the names of editors, as does *Literary Market Place.* Don't be penny wise and pound foolish by using an out-of-date reference. If your library doesn't have the current edition, buy it. It is money well spent. Or you can write to the Children's Book Council, 67 Irving Place, New York, NY 10003, and for a stamped, self-addressed envelope, they will send you a list of editors that is updated annually. And it is essential to take five minutes a week to look at *Publishers Weekly,* the trade journal for the publishing business. No picture book author can afford to miss its gossip column, "People," in which changes in personnel are announced as soon as they happen. The *Authors Guild Bulletin* and *School Library Journal* are also invaluable sources of information about staff changes. In writers' workshops, too, you can pick up news of who's buying what and who's working where—it's one of their important fringe benefits.

A call from a prospective writer who wants to describe his manuscript at length is simply an annoyance, but a call to confirm the spelling of the editor's name is considered professional and appropriate. This is especially important since a new editor or a recently promoted one is even more receptive to undiscovered talent than an editor with obligations to authors already firmly established on her list. There are exceptions to this general rule, however: (1) a publishing house that has had a temporary "freeze" on picture book acquisitions (and in these uncertain times, such "freezes" are common) might find itself short of manuscripts when the freeze is lifted, or (2) a publishing house may be attempting to change its editorial direction and be searching frantically for humorous texts, fantasy, or what-have-you to round out its traditional offering of, say, realistic stories or nonfiction.

Before you address your distinctive envelope to an editor, you should be sure that your manuscript is suited to his list. You do not do this in a long-winded long-distance phone call describing your storyline:

you do it in a number of ways, starting with studying the editor's requests for material in *Writer's Market,* checking the types of books issued by each publisher at the end of its *Literary Market Place* entry, and studying publishers' catalogs. Most publishers will cheerfully send you a copy of their latest catalog for the asking. One advantage of studying catalogs is that you can check the advertising copy for hints about the nature of the publisher's list. For instance, some publishers emphasize the "eternal" appeal of their new offerings; others underline the immediate and current appeal. Armed with this hidden information, you can tailor your covering letter to the publisher's taste.

If you are feeling impatient and don't want to wait the two months it can take to receive the catalog from the publisher, ask your librarian for a copy of *The Publishers' Trade List Annual.* This reference, which occupies two enormous volumes, is actually bound copies of publishers' catalogs. This is an important supplement to *Books in Print* and *Children's Books in Print.*

The largest customer for most children's picture books is still the library, both school and public. Although in these days of limited funds for new books you can't expect your local library to have *every* single book that has been published, you will find that enterprising librarians have a way of wangling copies of outstanding new books. Browsing through books new and old in the children's room of your local library is a valuable pastime. And a first-class bookstore will of course have all the latest books. Pore over them, and steep yourself thoroughly in all the books listed in the bibliography of this book. The books I have listed are ones I have discussed in these pages, but there are many, many other fine and exciting books. The more you read, the more you'll know—and if you don't have a wonderful time doing it, you probably should find another field! As you read and browse, be constantly aware of publishers' imprints. Try to analyze the trends in taste reflected in the books of various publishers, and when you have pinpointed two or three whose tastes seem to jibe closely with your own, you're ready to submit your manuscript to one of them.

The Query Letter

I am generally opposed to query letters. If you have done your homework, you don't need to ask an editor in advance whether she would be interested in a picture book subject. But I don't discourage writers from following their instincts. Sometimes a query letter makes sense. It is a rare picture book that is more than a thousand words long, for example. If you have written such a manuscript, it is probably a good idea to write to editors before you submit it, to ascertain whether

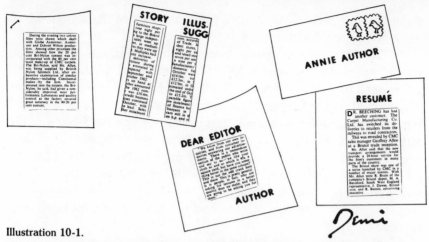

Illustration 10-1.

The submission package includes a stamped, self-addressed envelope, a dummy (with a decorated cover if you want to be a little creative!), a résumé, and two copies of the manuscript—one with the text double-spaced, the other including illustration suggestions alongside the text.

they would consider such a long book. Explain why the extra length is justified by the subject, and why you think the book will still hold your readers' attention.

The query letter can also give you some insight into the publisher's evaluation process. First, you will see how long it takes the publisher to answer your letter! It may take as long as evaluation of the manuscript itself, up to three months, because a description of a picture book manuscript can be difficult to decipher from a précis. Then, too, the letter you receive in reply will tell you something about the editor's approach.

The query letter has a legal advantage, too, which is useful if you plan to submit material that is valuable—a professionally typed manuscript or a dummy, or expensive photostats of sample illustrations. In writing a query letter, you are asking for a letter *requesting* that you send in your manuscript. This request protects you in the event that artwork or a dummy is lost, by putting the responsibility on the publisher.

But all things considered, as a picture book manuscript is so short, it makes sense to send it along with a covering letter without an advance query. In that covering letter, you can inform the editor that artwork or a dummy with pictures is available. A common beginner's mistake is to assume that a picture book manuscript has to be illustrated in order to be considered for publication. Nothing could be further from the truth. Picture book editors are expert visualizers, people who can see pictures through words, and any picture book editor will welcome the opportunity to consider the text on its own merits, independent of illustrative material. Most editors have a stable of illustrators whose work has appeal for their audience.

Never submit your manuscript with illustrations—you will cut your chances of acceptance in half. The editor may love the manuscript but reject it because he doesn't like the art. Or it can happen the other way around. Linda Glovach, the author-illustrator of *The Little Witch's Black Magic Cookbook,* got her start by illustrating a neighbor's manuscript. Kathryn Ernst, the editor who discovered Glovach in the slush pile, scrawled a note on the bottom of the rejection letter: "I like the art." Glovach appeared at the office with her portfolio a month later, and went on to create a successful series of holiday craft books. (Her success did not help her neighbor to get her manuscript published, however.)

Sometimes an editor is stumped. The manuscript is marvelous, but the illustration approach evades him. Bea Creighton, the editor of many classic picture books at Lothrop, Lee & Shepard, discovered a charming manuscript by Patricia Coombs about a little witch named Dorrie. She used Coombs's sketches for help in depicting the character, a disheveled little girl witch. Creighton was so delighted with the sketches that she asked Coombs to illustrate the book herself. But Coombs had to learn the demanding craft of preparing artwork for reproduction from production manager Stuart Benick before her sketches were accepted for publication. Today Coombs has a second career, illustrating not only her own books but others such as *Lobo and Brewster* by Gladys Yessayn Cretan. This is an exceptional case. Most of the time, the editor, with the assistance of his art director, welcomes the freedom of choosing an artist for a picture book without the author's help.

The editor has a lot of letters pouring in. Don't waste his time with chattiness! Be concise and to the point—in a word, be a pro. Your covering letter should never be more than a page long, and should tell something about why you have written the manuscript.

If your trial audiences have commented on the manuscript (beyond the dutiful "That's good, Mom"), you may want to share their reactions, briefly, with the editor. Point out anything that seems interesting and pertinent, but don't make a direct sales pitch for your book. It will speak for itself.

No matter how much an editor likes your writing style and approach, he is confined to some extent by the nature of his list. Only exposure to the overall offerings of a given publisher, supplemented by a close study of several of its recent children's picture books, will give you a sense of where your book belongs. It won't do, though, just to say, "I love everything you publish," because that gives the editor no insight into your taste and expectations. If you are able to say that you were deeply moved by a specific title, and that is why you are submitting your manuscript to that editor for consideration, the editor will appreciate the indirect compliment to his taste.

Your covering letter, then, has to address three major points: why you have written the book; how people who have seen it have reacted to it; and why you have chosen that particular publisher to evaluate it. You want to address these three points directly and succinctly, and that doesn't give you much room to talk about yourself.

The Résumé

You are an important selling point for your manuscript. The editor is interested in your experience with young children, your expertise in your subject area, your interests and avocations, and why you live where you live. Human interest has a universal appeal, and a short résumé about your personal professional life can help.

You don't have to be a world traveler or a widely published writer to capture the editor's attention. Your personality, as presented in your résumé, is bound to hold some interest. If you grew up in the Blue Ridge Mountains, if you have lived on the same block all your life, if you like to bowl, or if you spend your spare time volunteering in the library—such tidbits of information spark interest. If you are a professional working with children, you should mention this. If you have a special interest that has inspired you to try your hand at writing for a very young audience—hot-air ballooning or children's missions in China—mention that, too. You will want to cover your formal education, your writing history, and your work experience in separate paragraphs, but leave a little space for personal history and outside interests as well—they often say more about you than your professional achievements. And since picture book writing is such a personal expression, they're just as pertinent.

Like the covering letter, your résumé should be short—a page long at the most. Don't list every single article you have ever published: include only information that will help the editor "sell" you to the editorial committee and the sales staff.

The Manuscript

It is surprising how often manuscripts are submitted on notebook paper, or scrawled in an illegible hand. The manuscript you submit for consideration should be as ready for the typesetter as you can make it. It should be typed double-spaced with generous margins, page numbers on each manuscript page, and your name and address on each sheet in case the pages are separated (many writers use a rubber stamp). It's important that you present your manuscript professionally, so that it will be taken seriously. Editors have to read all day—and most

read all night as well—so careful typing and fresh paper make an important difference to tired eyes. Nothing is sadder than a manuscript that looks as if it's been through the washing machine, with rust marks from old paper clips and author's corrections scribbled in. It takes the magic away. Picture book writers struggle harder over each individual word than other writers, but they have the advantage of a manuscript that is short enough to retype easily when it begins to look bedraggled.

Sample Illustrations

If you think your illustration ideas are essential to the story, prepare a second copy of the manuscript with them included. Clever as your ideas may be, the editor still needs to evaluate your words separately. You can place illustration ideas in a contrasting color, such as red, facing the text allotted to that page, or you can cut up a carbon copy of the manuscript and paste it in place in the dummy. The first way is best for writers who are more comfortable with verbal descriptions, the second for the writer who isn't shy about his stick-figure indications. Don't struggle over your renderings, because the editor wants your ideas, not your final drawings. Your sketches will serve as a springboard for the illustrator the publisher commissions, and the more ambiguous you are, the better.

Collaborating with an artist before a manuscript is accepted is a dangerous proposition. First of all, as I noted earlier, you are doubling your chances of rejection. Then, if the editor decides to accept the manuscript without the art, or reject your manuscript and commission the artist for another project, you are risking the end of a beautiful friendship. Sometimes, though, the benefits of submitting art and words together outweigh the risks. If you and your friend the artist have a fabulous idea for a picture book that includes illustrations, don't let me talk you out of it. Many successful picture books have grown out of the inspired collaboration of friends and families. But if you submit your manuscript with pictures, be aware of these caveats:

1. Never submit artwork without a specific written request from the publisher.
2. Lay down the ground rules with your collaborator before you submit the manuscript.
3. Accept the fact that by submitting a complete package, you are cutting your chances for acceptance in half.

● **No professional writer submits artwork without a specific written request from the publisher.** Artwork is often unwieldy, so it may be tucked into a corner for safekeeping, only to be overlooked when you want it back. Publishers do not set out to lose artwork, but it does happen!

● **Lay down the ground rules with your collaborator.** It's a beautiful Sunday afternoon. You are taking a walk with a friend, and you hit upon a great idea for a children's book. You'll write the words, your friend will draw the pictures. High on inspiration, you never dream that this project could turn out any other way than perfectly. After months of individual work and mutual consultation, you submit the manuscript to a publishing house, and they want it. You are jubilant! Somewhere in the second paragraph, the editor gently rejects the artwork, suggesting that a famous artist has expressed interest in illustrating it in a somewhat different vein. Your euphoria evaporates. Your friend is hurt, and probably furious. When the friend is your husband or wife, or your child, the conflict is even more wrenching. Before anyone puts pen to paper, you should establish the rules for your collaboration. Discuss the possibilities before they become realities. Many collaborators split whatever offer they accept fifty-fifty, so that if only the words are accepted, the artist isn't left out in the cold. Others agree before the project starts to pay the artist for his time, so that if it doesn't work out, he's compensated. You can agree to submit it to ten publishers, or to take the first offer whatever its terms, but agree in advance.

● **Accept the fact that you are cutting your chances of acceptance in half by collaborating.** Unless you make it clear in your covering letter that the artwork and the manuscript can be considered independently, you risk rejection of the whole package on the basis of either the words or the pictures. Most editors have had at least one unpleasant experience with unhappy collaborators, so they are reluctant to become embroiled in half a project with two authors. If you just happened to collaborate, and each of you is going in a separate professional direction, explain this in your covering letter. If the project is just the way you both like it, stick to your guns until you have received rejection letters from ten publishers.

The Rejection Slip—Now What?

Thousands of manuscripts are submitted to publishers every year: writers are never allowed to forget that depressing fact. But there are also hundreds of publishers looking for manuscripts, and this fact is all too often forgotten. It's been said a thousand times before, but it needs repeating: editors are people, exercising personal taste. What appeals to one person may bore another. And an editor often turns down manuscripts that he likes very much, but for one reason and another aren't what he is looking for at the time.

These words are cold comfort to the writer confronted by a returned manuscript. The form rejection notice doesn't make it any easier. Frame it or toss it in the trash, but don't let it make you lose your faith in your work. Look your manuscript over, and consider whether you are still pleased with it. Does it need revision? Could it use a snappier beginning or a more conclusive ending? Pretend that you are the editor. How would you tell the author to improve it? If you can see constructive ways to change it, you might want to resubmit it to the same publisher. If you can't think of any way of improving it, and you think it has potential, send it elsewhere. Rare indeed is the writer who finds a publisher on the first go-round, although this happy ending is as enrapturing as love at first sight.

Multiple Submission

Many writers try to forestall this problem by submitting the manuscript to more than one publisher at a time. Ten years ago, multiple submission was considered a breach of etiquette, but today the practice is more and more widely accepted. A Xerox copy of a manuscript submitted with a personal covering letter can be received with the same enthusiasm as an original typescript. Many editors find the sharp black-and-white contrast of Xerox copies makes them easier to read than original typewritten copies. And a competitive instinct is set off by the prospect of another publisher reacting more quickly; this instinct works to the author's advantage. But the old school says, with validity, that a writer should give his chosen publisher a chance to evaluate the manuscript before letting the second-choice publisher have a crack at it. The matter of multiple submission is controversial—it's most sensible to follow your own hunch. If your manuscript is a topical one, multiple submission might make more sense than it would for a fantasy you have been working on for years.

If you submit your manuscript to ten publishers at once, and they all say it's not right for them, at least you haven't wasted any time finding out. (Comparing comments from publishers is one of the most illuminating ways to analyze your work, by the way.) Multiple submission becomes a problem when two publishers express interest. It's probably wisest to be up-front about the other publisher's interest as you negotiate: no editor is going to let a good manuscript get away because the competition agrees with his positive assessment!

Revising On Spec

Sometimes a publisher will ask you for your time and commitment before he offers you a contract. How should you handle this? *Should you have a cookie?* It depends. If you are hungry and dinner's three hours away, the answer is probably yes. If you've already had five cookies this afternoon and dinner's on the table, the answer is probably no.

Do you want a cookie? It depends. If the offer is oatmeal cookies and you can't stand raisins, the answer is most likely no. But if the offer is chocolate chip, your favorite, and your daughter made them herself, the answer might well be yes.

The question of revising a manuscript at the editor's suggestion, before a contract is offered, requires a similar thought process to obtain an answer.

Should you revise on speculation? It depends. If you still have enthusiasm for the manuscript, the answer might be yes. If you are immersed in a new project and don't want to break up your momentum, the answer could be no.

Do you want to revise on speculation? It depends. If the editor's suggestions make perfect sense, the answer could be yes. But if the editorial letter sounds routine, and the suggestions are pedestrian, the answer is most likely no.

Bear in mind that the majority of manuscripts revised on speculation never make it into print. Consider carefully whether the editor's suggestions make the manuscript *better,* or simply *different.* Also consider your objective: do you simply want to sell the manuscript, or are you interested in finding just the right publisher for it? Only you can juggle the answers to these questions and come up with the answer that fits. If you are still undecided, write your editor a note. Ask for a systematic clarification of his editorial advice. If he takes the time to give you a considered answer, you have some assurance of his interest.

I once worked with an author whose manuscript needed revision before I could propose it for publication. She sent me a letter explaining that she was taking sixteen teenagers to the World's Fair and finishing a novel for next season's publication, and that she would be free to consider my suggestions after she got back from Czechoslovakia eight months hence. I liked the manuscript, even though it wasn't quite right, so I got on the telephone and begged her to make time for the revisions before September. She laughed and confessed that her busy schedule was a product of her writer's imagination and that she would revise it right away now that she knew I was serious. It was a valuable lesson in the mutual regard editors and writers must have for one another in order to work effectively together.

To some writers, revision is painful and difficult work. To others, it is fun, because in their way of working, getting the words onto paper is the hard part. How you handle the different processes of writing, revising, selling, and maintaining your own integrity will form your decision about whether to revise on speculation.

11

Yes, We'd Like to Publish Your Manuscript

T he picture book author does not work in an ivory tower. His success has two very different requirements (almost diametrically opposed): (1) initially he must work alone, creating a strong manuscript; (2) to realize his initial conception he must be able to work amicably as a team with the editor, illustrator, designer, and art director. Once the picture book author understands that his writing is the framework for the contributions of others, he realizes that while his part in building a book is essential, it is incomplete. He must have the input of others. The rules of the game for this picture book team are spelled out in the contract.

The Contract

In studying a contract, your judgment must be based on the special requirements of the manuscript you are selling to determine which stipulations are unalterable and which can be negotiated. Too often, authors are so happy to be published that they close their eyes and sign the contract in a swoon. Occasionally, but also too often, an author will take the contract to a real estate lawyer or patent attorney who can raise all sorts of valid legal questions, not one of which is relevant to the terms of a publishing agreement. The sensible medium lies somewhere between these two extremes.

A publishing contract is a business agreement, not a dream come true. Like authors, publishers are usually honest, but not always. What protection does the author have? The basic and best protection is: Read your contract. Contracts don't follow any prescribed order, but there are certain conditions a wise author looks out for. As you read your contract, remember that the publisher *wants* to work with your project. Consider how much work your editor has put into a manuscript's becoming a book *before* the contract is offered. When you are offered a contract, you are in a solid, but not a spectacular, bargaining position. It is understood that you can take the manuscript elsewhere if the publisher does not meet your demands; it is also understood that the publisher can find satisfactory manuscripts from other sources if you are recalcitrant. Here are the crucial points contracts cover:

● **The Advance.** Publishers give authors a payment before the book is published as an advance against the royalties they will earn as the books are sold. A royalty is a percentage of the selling price—about 5 percent of the list price of the book. The author tends to believe that payment for his work is an affirmation of his professional status. This is absolutely true, but a picture book author's work is *not measured* by the size of the advance. Unlike adult books, which generally sell the most copies the first year, picture books get started slowly, then sell over a period of years. A picture book author may earn $80,000 in royalties over the course of his book's lifetime, but he will not be given an $80,000 advance as some adult authors are. His advances will start at about $1,000 and rise to about $5,000. Publishers usually base their advance payments on projected first-year sales, and for picture books these are usually relatively small. In the second year, after the book has been reviewed, picture book sales take off. Ask your editor how well she expects your book to sell, how long a period (a year, eighteen months, the first printing, the book's lifetime sales) the advance covers, and what kind of income you can expect in both the best and the worst projections. Armed with this information, you are in a position to consider whether your advance is fair.

● **Royalties.** Many first-time picture book authors are disappointed by the royalty rate they are offered. The most general practice is to split the royalties fifty-fifty between the author and the artist, so the picture book author has to expect to receive only half as much royalty as his peer the novelist. Another complicating factor is the high cost of producing a picture book as compared with an adult book or a book for older children—reinforced binding and sturdy paper selected for its good reproduction quality are expensive, and printing bills are extra high if color printing is used. In most cases, the author and artist bear the brunt of this expense: a publisher's rule of thumb is that the manufacturing cost per book (the cost of actually preparing, printing, and binding the book) plus the royalty should not exceed a quarter of the selling price. For this rule to be followed, it figures that if the manufacturing cost of the book is higher than average, the royalty must be lower than average. Nonetheless, a picture book writer's royalty should start at no lower than 5 percent of the list price of the book. After the first 10,000 copies are sold, most publishers are willing to raise the royalty to 6 or 7 percent. This sliding-scale royalty, beginning at a point where the publisher has recovered his initial investment and begins to make money on your book, makes sense all around, and you are justified in trying to hold out for it. Many writers urge the publisher to escalate the royalty again, to 7 or 8 percent, after 25,000 copies are sold. This is also an eminently fair arrangement, since a children's book that sells over 25,000 copies in hardcover editions these days is counted as a rousing success.

Paperback editions offer somewhat lower royalties, occasionally as little as half the royalty on the hardcover edition. The trick in negotiating a paperback royalty is to spell out a percentage based on the list price of the paperback edition. If it's only 3 or 4 percent, you're still getting a fair shake.

● **Subsidiary rights.** You won't impress your friends with these details of the contract as you will with the up-front money, but it is attention to these details that separates the professional from the bedazzled amateur.

People who are interested in reproducing your work in other forms will contact your publisher to make arrangements, logistical and financial. These other forms of your work are covered in the subsidiary rights section of your contract. Subsidiary rights are the licenses for the publication of the author's material in forms other than the publisher's edition. The publisher grants these licenses for a fee on the author's behalf. This is where the handful of rich authors get rich—through spectacular paperback sales; sales of serial rights to magazines; constant anthology use; foreign editions; filmstrip and movie sales; novelty use.

In most contracts, the publisher controls all the subsidiary rights to the picture book. This means that he is responsible for the sales of the book to other licensees, be they publishers, moviemakers, or book clubs. In most cases, the author's share of the subsidiary rights income is 25 percent, with another quarter going to the artist and half going to the publisher.

Anthology rights. Anthology rights include the publication of part or all of the manuscript in elementary school readers, children's literature textbooks, or any other books or magazines. The publisher who reprints your material, abridged, digested, or anthologized, pays a fee to the original publisher of your book. Your copyright appears on the copyright page of the book or magazine in which it appears.

Reprint. This is the republication of your material in its entirety by a publisher *other* than your original publisher. Most often, it pertains to paperback editions, but occasionally it applies to specially marketed hardcover editions. The content is identical to the original edition, but physical appearance may be slightly different (binding, paper, or type size).

Book clubs. Book clubs are as important to the children's book author as they are to adult authors. They reach audiences that publishers do not sell to directly. If Scholastic or Xerox or Troll takes your book on as a selection, it will be sold to children through flyers distributed in the classroom. The Junior Literary Guild sells hardcover editions to school libraries as well as directly to young customers. Book club advances range from $500 to $5,000 on the average.

First and second serial rights. In contracts, magazine arrangements are usually spelled out under "First Serial" (publication in a periodical prior to publication) and "Second Serial" (publication in a magazine after the book is available to the general public). Historically, first serial rights were valuable—readers eager for the next Fitzgerald novel would snap up the *Saturday Evening Post* for an advance peek. These rights were sold at enormous prices, because people could buy the magazine at a tenth of the cost of a book, and this cut into book sales. These sales were rarely important in children's book publishing, and today first serial rights are considered much less valuable even for adult books. Now they are often sold for very little because it's assumed they offer good publicity. Except for the occasional sensational White House memoir, these rights are not much in demand. Second serial rights are of far greater interest to today's picture book writer because a number of periodicals, such as *Cricket,* regularly purchase second serial rights to picture books. This gives the editors of the magazine that will serialize the book the opportunity to evaluate the published book. Again, these rights are sometimes sold for very little, because the publicity value is so great. A conscientious publisher will keep trying assiduously to have a book serialized or featured in magazines, because the exposure and the income benefit both publisher and author.

Movie. The average picture book is too short to make into a feature film, though you never know what an enterprising and imaginative producer will consider movie material. Picture books are often adapted for filmstrips, however, by companies like Weston Woods and ERC, for use in schools and public libraries. While the money paid for these filmstrips is minuscule compared to Hollywood deals, filmstrips are enjoying increasing popularity, and advances and royalty payments should enjoy a similar rise.

Foreign. Foreign sales are more important to the picture book author than any other kind of sale. If you figure that it costs $10,000 more to manufacture a picture book than a "standard" book, you will understand why so many publishers say to authors, "We'd love to publish your book, but first we must see if we can arrange a coproduction." A coproduction is an arrangement wherein the costs of producing, printing, and binding are shared between publishers of different countries. For instance, an American publisher would send a manuscript and sample art to publishers in England, Japan, France, Germany, and Sweden, and these publishers might agree that they wanted to publish the book at the same time as the American publisher. Contracts would be drawn up, and instead of a 10,000-copy first printing for the American market alone, a 50,000-copy printing could be arranged for all the countries concerned. This is an ideal arrangement, and an increasingly viable one. Every April, publishers of picture books from all over the world gather at the Bologna Book Fair in Italy to show each other new projects and to discuss the possibilities of producing books together.

Once a picture book is published, foreign coproducers help it stay in print. They may add five years to the life of the book. Once a book has been in print a while, it is usually uneconomical to reprint the standard two or three thousand copies of a picture book needed to fill orders. Foreign coproducers can double, triple, even quadruple that number.

The advance and royalty involved in foreign editions are relatively small compared with the American deal. They are roughly half the original advance and royalty. Under most contracts, this amount is divided equally between the author and artist. A standard picture book contract by an American publisher for a foreign edition includes an advance of about a thousand dollars. The publisher takes half of this ($500), leaving the author with a quarter ($250) and the illustrator with a quarter ($250). However, the prestige and the expanded market are of great value. Also, the larger the quantity of a book that is published, the lower the production cost. Therefore the price of the American edition is made low enough to appeal to a wider audience on the home front.

If an editor proposes that your manuscript be shown to foreign publishers before he offers you a contract, jump at the chance. Foreign publishers who look at projects can offer valuable insights into your work. A Japanese publisher can reject it as "too wordy," the English publisher might call it "too slight," the French publisher might find that it is "not personal enough," the German publisher might find the art "too simple," and the Swedish publisher would accept it because it is "so up-to-date." The insights of individual international publishers help focus a book for the American market, and often a small change can make it more widely accepted.

Subsidiary Rights Checklist

Subsidiary rights have changed drastically in the last 20 years. New technologies present opportunities for writers who study the fine print of this clause carefully.

— Abridgement

— Anthology rights

— Digest rights

— First serialization

— Cartoon strip

— Radio

— Television

— Video cassette

— Cable television

— Film strip

— Movie

— Foreign rights
  To distribute in English
  To translate into other languages

— Transcription
  Records
  Recordings and accompanying Braille texts

— Reprint rights in cheap editions
  (paperback)

— Reprint rights in special editions
  (often aimed at libraries)

● **Copyright.** Anyone who reads is familiar with that fearsome caveat that appears on the copyright page of every book: *All rights reserved. No part of this book may be reproduced, stored in a retrieval system, or transmitted in any form or by any means, electronic, mechanical, photocopying, recording or otherwise without prior written permission of the publisher.*

When your book is published, some version of this notice will appear under your copyright. It protects you and the artist and your publisher from unauthorized editions or reprintings of your work.

Copyright also protects you from plagiarism. Under copyright, the precise expression of your idea is considered your own, and anyone who copies you, word for word, is guilty of plagiarism. Unfortunately for authors, the judgments against plagiarizers are usually token amounts, and even when the plagiarism seems obvious to you, it has to be a brazen theft of your every word to move a court of law. You would be lost without copyright protection, so your contract has to include provisions for the copyright. It may surprise you to know that it doesn't matter in whose name the copyright is taken, so long as it is registered with the Library of Congress. Some publishers take the copyright in their own name, just to simplify clerical matters. The contract spells out the arrangement between you and the publisher, and indicates who retains the rights to the story once the book is out of print. So it doesn't matter to you in whose name the copyright is taken, so long as it is thoroughly covered in the contract.

Most publishers are set up to take care of all the copyright information and follow-up; it's your responsibility to provide them with your full name and birth date (to keep them from confusing you with another copyright holder of the same name) when the copyright is registered. Some publishers are so well mechanized in this area that they will send you a card along with your contract asking for the information that is pertinent to registering a copyright.

● **Publisher's indemnity clause.** Whenever a successful book is published, it's almost axiomatic that someone believes that his or her idea has been pirated. It is astonishing how many lawsuits, threatened and actual, come to the attention of publishers. Though these suits are far more common in adult publishing, the standard indemnity clause, guaranteeing that the work being purchased for publication is the writer's own and that if the publisher is sued for the infringement of another copyright the author will pay for the damages, is included in picture book contracts. It is practically impossible to talk a publisher out of this clause, so most picture book writers are content to sign their initials to it, knowing full well that it will never affect the course of their book.

● **Option clause.** The option clause used to be sacred, the legal bond between the loyal author and his devoted publisher. Like the manual typewriter, the option clause has had its day. If your contract contains an option clause, which gives your publisher first refusal on your next book project, suggest to your editor that it be deleted. Many editors will sigh and then agree to strike it. If your editor insists on leaving it in, discuss how it can be modified. If you have written a picture book about a pet squirrel named Molly, offer the publisher the option to publish a sequel about this same squirrel. If that tack fails, suggest that they be given the option to publish your next nonfiction picture book about squirrels. If that fails, offer your next nonfiction picture book, in proposal form. If your publisher won't accept this, finally offer them your next nonfiction picture book. But do not give your publisher carte blanche on whatever you write next. It's a dangerous agreement—and it could end up in a legal battle.

Many authors willingly sign a contract with an option clause, and when the time comes to submit the second manuscript, they dig an old manuscript out of the desk drawer and submit it believing that no publisher would accept it. But a book contract is a business agreement, and you want your option clause to be meaningful. Tailor your option clause to your needs, and your publisher's. Make certain that if you do sign an option clause, it is as specific as possible; that it includes a cutoff date for the publisher to exercise his option; that the book to which the publisher has first refusal is carefully described; and that it specifies in what form you are to submit this second project.

The option clause can work to the author's advantage as well as the publisher's, but it should be worded precisely and discussed thoroughly before you sign your name to it.

● **Other clauses of interest.** The details of publishing a book are often written into a contract. If you are concerned that it may take ten years for the illustrator the editor has chosen to complete the pictures, you may want to ask that there be a limit to the time the publisher has to publish the book. Most often this is eighteen months after the delivery and approval of the final manuscript. If after those eighteen months the illustrations are not ready, you have the right—but not the obligation—to withdraw the book and take it elsewhere.

Approvals—of the illustrations, of the jacket and jacket flap copy, of the advertising copy—are also occasionally written into contracts. If you have a good working relationship with your editor, such approvals are probably unnecessary, but some writers are more comfortable knowing that those rights are guaranteed in the contract. Especially when a writer has had experience with publishing, so that his input has value, it makes sense to include guarantees of approvals.

Revision is discussed—with all its ramifications—in the next chapter.

Contracts puzzle everyone, even seasoned professionals, so there are many organizations devoted to helping authors know what is a fair contract and what is not so fair. The Authors Guild, 23 W. 43rd St., New York, NY 10036, offers valuable pamphlets and advice on contracts, constantly updated to keep the writer informed about changes taking place in the current marketplace. Your writer friends and local writers' workshops are also invaluable aids in finding out what you should agree to and what you shouldn't.

The contract checklist on the following page gives you an idea of what should be covered in your contract. The more things are spelled out, the less likely there is to be trouble later. How the points are covered is a matter to be discussed between you and your editor, but it's your job to insist that everything is covered.

A rule of thumb for picture book writers: your contract should be at least twice as long as your manuscript!

Contract Checklist

One of the most troublesome things about contracts is the important matters that are left out. Be sure that the points below are amplified fully in your contract before you sign it.

__ Advance
>first payment
>second payment
>third payment

__ Royalties
>first 10,000 copies
>second 10,000 copies
>copies sold thereafter

__ Indemnity clause

__ Reversion-of-rights clause

__ Delivery date

__ Publication date

__ Approvals
>text
>advertising copy
>illustrations

Provisions for semiannual royalty statements

__ Provisions for audit of publisher's books

__ Provision that all subsidiary rights not specifically mentioned in contract remain the property of the author

__ Grant of rights
>world rights in English
>foreign languages

__ Provisions for correcting galleys

12

Do I Need an Agent?

Oh, I never worry about the details of my contracts," says Charles Keller, author of picture books of jokes and riddles, including *Too Funny for Words* and *Ballpoint Bananas.* Like many prolific and established writers, Keller has an agent. "My agent takes care of that so that I can worry about what actually goes into the books themselves." His agent gets quick attention for his new projects, does the legwork, handles wearisome packing-up and postage-paying details, uses her reputation and relationships with editors to place his manuscripts—and negotiates a better contract than he could negotiate himself. This leaves Keller free to concentrate on the actual writing problems that face any author.

In exchange for this array of services, his agent gets 10 percent of all the money Keller earns on the books she sells for him: 10 percent of his advance, 10 percent of his royalties, 10 percent of all subsidiary rights sales, and 10 percent of any movie arrangements. For Keller, she's worth every penny and more.

The picture book agent knows a great deal about this narrow slice of the publishing world. Her concerns are for the financial health and growing reputation of her clients, as any agent's are, but her actions are specially tailored to the needs of the field. She understands the complexities of production schedules, the importance of prizes to sales, and the peculiar writing demands of the picture book manuscript. She is not so concerned with Hollywood connections and multimillion-dollar paperback deals as she is with the steady output and continuing excellence of her authors as creators of picture books. She knows that picture book customers are experts, and that her authors must not let them down.

Few agents of any kind are willing to take on an unpublished client, and especially rare is the experienced agent who is willing to take on an unpublished client in the picture book field. Simple arithmetic explains this. Advances for picture book manuscripts are small: around $1,000 for a newcomer, up to $3,000 or $4,000 for someone with an established track record. With no greater effort than it takes to make less than $500, then, the agent could sell a novel for $10,000 or $20,000 and up. Lunch with a children's book editor is just as time-consuming as lunch with an adult editor. A telephone call to a picture book author costs just as much as a call to a novelist and takes the same amount of time. An agent trying to make a living can always find ways to make better money than by selling children's picture books. All this adds up to the near impossibility of an unpublished author finding an agent to handle his picture book.

But children's picture books have the same appeal to agents as they do to writers. Max Becker, a well-known New York agent, doesn't handle children's books anymore, but when he was just starting out importing European books he handled Saint-Exupéry's *The Little Prince,* a source of great pride—and income—for him to this day. Carol Mann, who started her publishing career as a juvenile editor, still loves children's books and handles a few picture book writers. A few, because the time involved in selling and negotiating contracts for picture books is clearly a luxury for an agent trying to make a living.

The two agents best known for their work with children's picture books are Dorothy Markinko and Marilyn Marlowe. Different as they are in style and background, Markinko and Marlowe share an ardent devotion to the cause of children's books. And they are busy. Each handles more than a hundred clients, writers whose names you would recognize instantly and whose output is prolific, lucrative, and of the highest quality. Neither is actively looking for new clients, no matter how talented, because they are fully committed to the talent they represent now.

Markinko, a former editor herself, represents such well-known clients as Dick Gackenbach, Daniel Manus Pinkwater, and Patricia Coombs. She reads and reads and reads. Even though her clients have proven track records, she protects their careers by suggesting that a weak story could be put aside for a while, or rewritten. "Always read a manuscript from Dorothy Markinko carefully," Edna Barth of Lothrop, Lee & Shepard used to tell me when I was a junior editor. "She never sends over anything that isn't publishable."

Marlowe, a longtime agent with a reputation for excellence, enjoys the same credibility with editors. "I study the market," Marlowe says, "and the success I have had is the result of watching very carefully. Children's picture books are specially marketed, so that I have to study every clause of the contract carefully. I compare a publisher's promises with royalty statements from his house from previous years. I go through every contract as carefully as an editor goes through a manuscript."

Is an Agent for You?

The literary agent is most valuable to the *established* writer who does not want to sully his relationship with his editor with arguments over royalty rates or foreign-rights splits. An agent can help a writer who is making a substantial income from his writing with tax advice, ammunition against writer's block, and new contacts. These are services that a promising new writer doesn't need yet. And the one service an agent cannot provide is selling an unsalable manuscript.

Selling a manuscript is only a tiny part of an agent's job. It is an essential part of the process, but agents generally handle only manuscripts that are salable. The agent is primarily concerned with selling the manuscript on the terms most favorable to the author, and this is possible only when he has a proven sales and review record to work with. Only when a publisher has expressed interest in buying the manuscript does the agent's real work start.

Ironically, as a new writer you have a better chance of selling your book *without* an agent. Your contract for that first book may not end up in the Authors Guild Hall of Fame for its generous terms and large advance, but it gets your foot in the door! Agents are interested in setting precedents for future contracts, and it is just possible that an agent's professional standards for an acceptable contract won't—and can't—be met by a publisher on a first book by an unknown author. With the second book, you'll have learned from experience, and can represent yourself more forcefully.

If you do your homework, and ask for help from the Authors Guild, the Society of Children's Book Writers, and local writers' groups, you will be able to handle your own contract negotiations for the first few books. After you have proved to yourself and the world that you are seriously interested in this form, then it is time to think about finding an agent.

Finding an Agent

Finding an agent is a tough business, even with a few books under your belt. Most writer-agent arrangements are based on a handshake, not a formal contract. Writer and agent have a close relationship, with all the pleasures and tensions of any partnership. If the agent hasn't been able to sell the writer's last three manuscripts, he naturally tends to explain it as a failure on the writer's part. The writer, of course, wonders if the agent is doing a conscientious job. The pressures of survival for both agent and writer can create explosive situations. And sometimes agents and writers part company on less than friendly terms. The informality of the original agreement between writer and agent

keeps the matter out of court. Many writers are frustrated by their editors' reluctance to take sides in writer-agent disputes. Editors have close relationships with agents, as they do with writers. Most publishing houses have a strict policy of neutrality when inevitable differences of opinion arise.

Choosing the right agent is one of the most constructive steps you can take in your writing career, and choosing a wrong agent can be disastrous. Since you will be working long and closely with your agent, it's a good idea to interview him before you commission him to sell your book. If you can't meet him in person, ask him to set aside a half-hour to talk to you on the telephone. Find out who his other clients are. Ask him about recent sales. Talk to him about writers you admire, and books you have enjoyed. Discuss which publishers he likes to work with. If you don't like the answers he's giving you, let him know. Listen to what he says, and look between the lines. Your agent is the person you will turn to when your book goes out of print, when Walt Disney makes a six-figure offer for the movie rights, when a pirated edition of your book turns up at a book fair. You have to trust him, and it helps if you like him, too.

Agenting is a business, and as you look for an agent, you should bear this in mind. Unable to read all the manuscripts that come across their desks, enterprising agents have invented the "reading fee." Sometimes this is money well spent, but be sure you know what you are paying for when an agent offers to review your work for a price.

For picture book manuscripts, the reading fee usually ranges from $25 to $50. If you want an opinion from a person who doesn't know you, this service can be useful. But bear in mind that most big literary agencies that offer this service have a special reading staff. The people on this staff are usually *not* the agents who sell manuscripts. They are teachers or writers or journalists making a little extra money on the side. They might know less about children's picture book writing than you do.

Some agents who offer a reading service will consider representing you if the reader's judgment of your manuscript is positive. If they are able to sell the manuscript—and it does happen—they will deduct the reading fee from the standard agent's percentage of your advance. This is certainly a fair arrangement, protecting your time and the agent's. Be sure, though, that it is spelled out in writing before you go ahead with such a deal.

The "personalized letters" from some of the larger agencies can swell your ego, but only until you discover you've been had. If you receive a letter implying you have potential and suggesting that the agent read your manuscript for a fee, write back:

Dear Mr. Agent:

Thank you for your letter about my manuscript, *One Dark Night*. I would like to work with you in revising and marketing it, on the condition that you will deduct the reading fee from my advance as part of your agent's commission, once the manuscript is sold. If this arrangement is satisfactory to you, please let me know.

I think it's fair for an agent to charge a reading fee, for a thoughtful reading of a manuscript requires skill and attention. But there's no point in having your manuscript read by someone who may have no intention of selling it, unless you have decided beforehand that this is what you want. For this kind of reading, you are probably better off with a writing school, a workshop, or a course in children's literature.

The Lawyer Agent

Some writers, once they have proven to themselves that they are serious, find that they are more comfortable having a lawyer handle their affairs with publishers. If you are from an area where the literary agent population is sparse, you may be tempted to settle for the local lawyer, when a literary agent without a law degree could represent you far more effectively. There are several well-known literary lawyers who represent some top picture book creators, but they are as highly specialized as brain surgeons. A literary lawyer would be at sea at your house closing, and a real estate lawyer is not going to be very happy, or competent, negotiating your book contract. If you have to make a choice, you are probably better off with a nonlawyer literary agent than you are with a nonliterary lawyer. All agents formalize their relationship with an author through the book contract.

The Agent and Your Contract

Agents are included in the contract for the book they represent. In the standard publishing contract, there is a clause specifying that the publisher should pay money to the agent as a legal discharge of its financial responsibility to the author. This works to everyone's advantage, because it means the agent can check the royalty statement, deduct his fee, and send a check to the writer in one simple move.

The writer does not have to become embroiled in money matters, a real relief when he has dozens of books in print.

More and more agents are insisting that the agent clause in the publishing contract be amended to specify that the agent will be sent his money directly for as long as that book is in print with that publisher.

There is nothing wrong with this setup, but if you have any doubts about your agent, you should be aware of the extent of your commitment.

Traditionally, the writer has been free to dismiss his agent at any time during a book's life. If a writer was unhappy with his agent, all he had to do was write to the publisher and request that all monies be sent directly to him, or through another agent of his choice. These days, the best agents protect their professional integrity by writing into the contract an alliance that will endure as long as the book does. Once the contract is signed, disputes between the writer and his agent can be settled only in court. This is serious stuff, so think about it carefully first.

In the children's book field, an agent won't help you get your foot in the door. If you are good, and are writing manuscripts worthy of publication, picture book editors will find you in the slush pile. If your writing is not up to snuff, the most prestigious agent in the business can't sell your stories. To the established author, an agent is an enthusiastic fan, a determined cheerleader, and a valued colleague for the writer who doesn't need the distractions of contracts and money matters. As your career develops, you will depend increasingly on the business acumen and the stalwart support a good agent offers.

The following list is a personal one, of agents I've worked with and know. The nonappearance of any agent on this list has no significance of any kind: no agent works with every single publisher. If you want to get in touch with any of these agents with an eye to having them represent you, submit a letter to them before you submit any manuscripts. This letter should describe the projects you are trying to sell, as well as a paragraph or two about your experience and qualifications. Always include a stamped, self-addressed envelope along with your letter so that you will be sure of getting an answer. Many of these agencies only handle an occasional picture book manuscript, so don't allow yourself to be discouraged by negative responses. Just keep trying!

Maxwell Aley Associates
145 East 35th Street
New York, N.Y. 10016

Julian Bach Literary Agency
3 East 48th Street
New York, N.Y. 10017

Georges Borchardt, Inc.
136 East 57th Street
New York, N.Y. 10022

Curtis Brown Ltd.
575 Madison Avenue
New York, N.Y. 10022

Jane Jordan Browne
170 South Beverly Drive
Beverly Hills, Calif. 90210

Ruth Cantor
156 Fifth Avenue
New York, N.Y. 10010

Collier Associates
280 Madison Avenue
New York, N.Y. 10016

Richard Curtis Literary Agency
156 East 52nd Street
New York, N.Y. 10022

Jay Garon-Brooke Associates
415 Central Park West
New York, N.Y. 10025

International Creative Management
40 West 57th Street
New York, N.Y. 10019

Alex Jackinson
55 West 42nd Street
New York, N.Y. 10036

Bertha Klausner
71 Park Avenue
New York, N.Y. 10016

Lenniger Literary Agency
457 Fifth Avenue
New York, N.Y. 10016

Barbara Lowenstein
250 West 57th Street
New York, N.Y. 10019

McIntosh and Otis
475 Fifth Avenue
New York, N.Y. 10017

Carol Mann
168 Pacific St.
Brooklyn, N.Y. 11201

Toni Mendez
140 East 56th Street
New York, N.Y. 10022

Scott Meredith Literary Agency
845 Third Avenue
New York, N.Y. 10022

Robert P. Mills
156 East 52nd Street
New York, N.Y. 10022

Nicholas Literary Agency
161 Madison Avenue
New York, N.Y. 10016

Ray Peekner
2625 North 36th Street
Milwaukee, Wis. 53210

Raines and Raines
475 Fifth Avenue
New York, N.Y. 10017

Kim Rosston
246 West End Avenue
New York, N.Y. 10023

Russell and Volkening
551 Fifth Avenue
New York, N.Y. 10017

Frances Schwartz, Literary Agency
60 East 42nd Street
New York, N.Y. 10017

Rita Scott, Inc.
25 Sutton Place
New York, N.Y. 10022

Evelyn Singer Agency Inc.
Box 163
Briarcliff Manor, N.Y. 10510

Writers House
132 West 31st Street
New York, N.Y. 10001

13

From Manuscript to Finished Book

The editorial office of a publishing company houses more than editors. A typical children's book staff is made up of type designers, art directors, production editors, and copyeditors as well as the chief editor, senior editors, associate editors, assistant editors, and editorial assistants. When your manuscript arrives at the publishing office, it is usually opened, acknowledged, and skimmed by the editorial assistant, who typically passes it on to the assistant editor in charge of reading through the manuscripts, reporting in detail on those that seem to hold some promise, and assigning inappropriate manuscripts to a rejection pile. The editor-in-chief is often the only other person who sees this rejection pile. Edna Barth, editor-in-chief at Lothrop, Lee & Shepard and an author herself, never let a manuscript go back to the author until she had looked it over herself. Many sensitive editors subscribe to this policy, because the experienced eye can pick out the manuscript that has hidden possibilities despite glaring flaws like lengthiness or incongruous characterization.

The promising manuscripts selected by the assistant editor are read and discussed by other editors on the staff. Many houses have an editorial board where the majority opinion holds. In other houses, a manuscript needs only one champion, a single editor who is willing to take a chance—sometimes even stake his job—on a manuscript.

Illustration 13-1.

As your book goes through the selection, editing and production processes, you will meet many members of the publishing company's staff.

In James Daugherty's *Andy and the Lion*, the author-illustrator uses a lion-yellow wash over his inspired line drawing in this example of two-color (black is one color, yellow the second color) artwork.

One-color illustrations needn't be printed in black, as this illustration from Robert McCloskey's *Blueberries for Sal* shows. It is printed in a dark blue, which creates readable type and a visual mood appropriate to the story.

Aunt Bessie always said they both did very neat embroidery. But Annabelle thought that Nellie's stitches were really a little bit neater.

Hand separation is an art in which the illusion of color is created with skillful combinations of limited color. Here author-artist Dale Payson uses black, red, and yellow to show a rich spectrum in *Almost Twins*, a story of sibling rivalry set at the turn of the century.

Barbara Cooney uses bright swatches of color to simulate a medieval painting in her Caldecott Medal-winning picture book, *Chanticleer and the Fox*. She uses four colors—black, red, yellow, and blue—and each color is painted on a separate overlay for maximum control over the reproduction quality in the finished book.

Thomas B. Allen sketched this layout for his final drawings of Rosa in *Where Children Live.* The layout reflects the author's concern that the illustrations show the interior of her home, as well as an outdoor picture.

ROSA lives beside a river in Nicaragua. The roof of her house is made of palm fronds. Bananas grow on trees in her yard and orchids grow wild in the jungle nearby. Two parrots fly past her window every morning.

ROSA

lives beside a river in Nicaragua. The roof of her house is made of palm fronds. Bananas grow on trees in her yard and orchids grow wild in the jungle nearby. Two parrots fly past her window every morning.

The finished illustration of Rosa in *Where Children Live* deviates somewhat from the rough layout, but the artist has retained the general composition and editorial content in his final painting.

Much preliminary work goes into
the preparation of illustrations.
Here are samples from Thomas
B. Allen's illustration of Nils
in *Where Children Live*. Some
of the sketches anticipate the final
paintings; others are explorations
of the subject that the artist
discarded later.

This final painting of Nils shows how the artist's ideas have coalesced, with each carefully chosen detail in place.

FOUR-COLOR PROCESS PRINTING   ROTATION OF COLORS

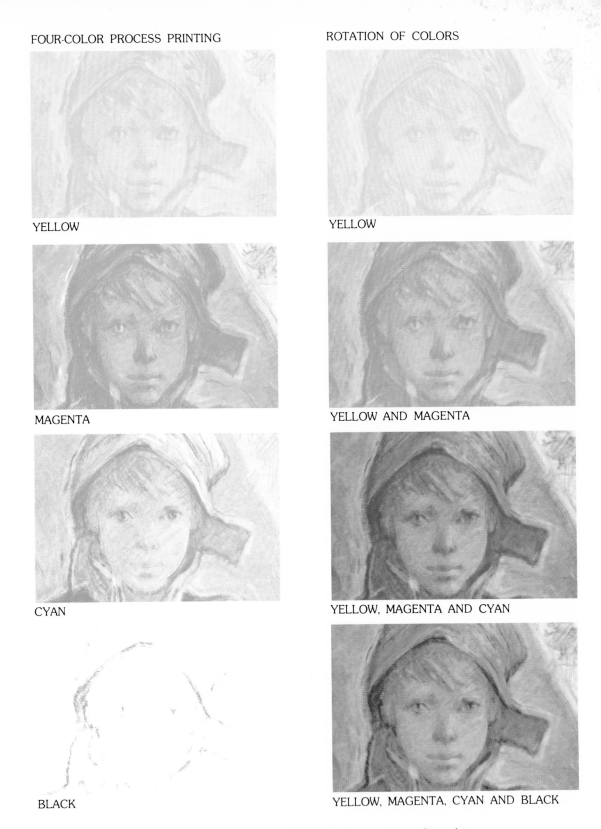

YELLOW

YELLOW

MAGENTA

YELLOW AND MAGENTA

CYAN

YELLOW, MAGENTA AND CYAN

BLACK

YELLOW, MAGENTA, CYAN AND BLACK

This detail from Thomas B. Allen's *Where Children Live* is printed in the
component colors and then the final composite to show how the four-color
printing process works. The camera-separated artwork is printed in the four
so-called process colors: black, yellow, cyan and magenta.

The Editorial Process

Once a manuscript is accepted and put under contract, it is assigned to an editor. The editor's job is to read your manuscript as the reader will—to judge the writing on its own merits. Authors are sometimes touchy about being assigned to a junior editor, but in fact, this is often an advantage. Lack of experience often also means freshness, and the absence of other commitments allows a degree of personal attention that is relatively hard to come by with busy senior editors. The duties of any editor, junior or senior, are so many and so varied that the actual editing of manuscripts is a small, though cherished, part of his job. He has to attend meetings, write letters and memos, keep his filing up-to-date, answer his ever-ringing telephone, and perhaps lunch with agents several times a week. But when an editor does find the peace and quiet to edit your manuscript, he approaches it with a single-mindedness and objectivity that can be startling to an author. Unlike your friendly neighbor or enthusiastic writing teacher, he will soon sniff out spots that could be expressed a little more smoothly, twists of the plot that could be effected more succinctly or dramatically, or characterizations that the illustrations could portray, eliminating the need for so much description. Editors are word people. They respect writers who are concerned about their manuscripts after they are sold, and find it thrilling to watch writers learn and develop as their books undergo the editing and production process. The best way to get to know your editor and his style is to write to him. Editorial advice differs with editorial personalities. There are cheery editors who demand a total rewrite; there are gruff editors who are fierce in their criticism, and end up asking for only small changes. So it does help to know your editor, and it's worth the extra time to write out your questions and objections.

Once the editor has suggested structural changes, more felicitous wordings, and general tightening, he turns his attention to illustration. The standards for illustration differ with the kind of book involved. In a storybook, the editor looks for contrast, excitement, suspense. In an informational book, he looks for consistency, even pacing, and scale. In a concept book, he will strive to keep the presentation of ideas on each page and each double-page spread the same size, so that the reader is never bored by too little action or jolted by surprising jumps from idea to idea. The editor has an instinct, honed by exposure and experience, for overall tone. He knows how the different elements of the picture book combine to create a whole that is true to your story, appropriate to the illustrations, and appealing to the audience.

The editor's allies in developing the book's illustratability are the art director and the type designer. The art director is usually a commercially trained artist with experience in the peculiarities of book making.

An important part of the art director's job is to look over artists' portfolios, so that when an editor brings her a manuscript, she has several names to suggest. The editor usually narrows down the choices to two or three prime candidates. The art director sends the manuscript to these illustrators, often asking them for sketches or a sample illustration to see if their interpretation is in keeping with your intentions and the editor's.

Layout and Illustration

When the illustrator is finally selected, he creates a dummy book with rough illustrations along with a single *comp*—a comprehensive color illustration that gives everybody a pretty good idea of what the look of the book will be. At no point in the making of a book are an author's tact and diplomacy so tested as at this stage. Of course you had a clear mental image of how your book would look—if you didn't have a strong visual sense, you'd be writing newspaper articles or novels. But your job in reviewing the rough illustrations is a technical one, where personal taste has to be put aside. Are the characters the right age? Does the house change color from page 4 to page 8 without explanation? Is the grackle the right shape? Are the eight ducks you specified in the text all in the picture? If you are helpful, polite, and appreciative, your editor will remember. If you are critical, opinionated, and openly disappointed, he won't forget when you offer him your next book.

Next the illustrator and the type designer meet to discuss the layout of the book. Type design is one of the most important, and most underrated, aspects of book production. In children's picture books, the choice of typography can make or break a well-written manuscript and beautiful pictures.

When the type designer and the illustrator have agreed on a typeface, a small part of the manuscript is set in sample pages, to give everyone a chance to comment on the type choice. (You should ask to see them, because an author can sometimes offer insights that an art staff overlooks. Margot Tomes, an inspired and experienced illustrator, once corrected a *New York Times* reviewer who had complimented the illustrator's clever use of typography in *Everyone Is Good for Something* by Beatrice Schenk de Regniers. "The placement of the typography was the author's idea re placing bits of type around simple little pictures, not mine," Tomes pointed out.)

On the next two pages, you will see some of the subtleties the type designer, illustrator, editor, and author must deal with to make the book readable and attractive to your beginning-reader audience. The illustrator may suggest cutting a line or two to make a splashier picture, you may want to change a line of dialogue to fit the character the illus-

has brought into focus for you, or the editor may want to change a comma to a dash to emphasize a point.

Dotting the I's and Crossing the T's

Now the book is ready for copyediting, the final step in preparing a manuscript for typesetting. Some editors copyedit the manuscripts they have edited. Others feel that a fresh eye is essential to the success of a manuscript that has been so much discussed and revised. What the copyeditor does is to make sure that your grammar is correct, that your telling is consistent, that those words that everybody knows how to spell are not somehow spelled incorrectly. The copyeditor is the guardian of precision, the protector of facts, a professional perfectionist dedicated to the idea that you can believe what you read.

Authors and copyeditors get along about as well as children and dentists. A good copyeditor wields his drill with delicacy and skill, but sometimes it hurts. "She has edited the heart and life out of my manuscript," one author sputtered to me over the phone. When I quoted the complaint to my demon copyeditor, she replied simply, "I told you he was redundant." It was true, but I could sympathize with the author's wrath. If you sometimes feel antagonistic toward your copyeditor, you're in good company—but like fillings and root canals, the copyeditor's changes are for your own good. And of course a given alteration is always reversible; provided you can convince your editor your way is better! But be sure you *are* right, and beware of playing fast and loose with a copyedited manuscript. It's fatally easy to introduce new errors in tampering at this stage.

Galleys

After the sample pages and the rough illustrations are approved, the copyedited text is set into galley proofs. Most contracts are very specific about an author's involvement with galleys. Typically, you will be given two weeks to look them over, and to make corrections to bring them into conformity with the manuscript you and the editor approved. Two kinds of changes are made in galleys: corrections of printer's errors, called PEs in publishing jargon, and author's alterations, or AAs. A mistake is a mistake, you say, but there is a crucial difference between the two: the printer, or more precisely the typesetter, pays for PEs, and *you* pay for AAs. If you think that changing "he thought" to "he mused" is a stroke of genius, go ahead and do it, but remember you are paying about ten dollars for *every* line you change. This can add up! Editors, too, have been known to have last-minute brainstorms to make a good manuscript perfect, and many authors are unaware that

The Author's Guide to

The words are yours and type is the medium used to convey these words to the reader. The right typeface can enhance your concepts and embellish the appearance of your book. It is the job of the designer to make those choices that would most effectively convey your meaning. To give you a sense of what the designer deals with, the following is a general description of the most used typographic terms:

Melior

Optima

Palatino

Serif
Gothic

Bodoni

Caslon

Bauhaus
Demi

Benquiat

Baskerville

Caledonia

Ascender—The part of a lowercase letter above the x-height

Baseline—The line on which the characters appear to stand

Characters—Individual letters, figures and punctuation marks

Counter—The enclosed or hollow part of a letter

Descender—The part of a lowercase letter that falls below the baseline

Em—A printer's unit of width measurement which is equal to the body size of the type in question. An 8-point em is 8 points; a 14-point em is 14 points, etc. It takes its name from the widest letter in any typeface: M.

Font—A complete alphabet: one typeface in one size

Italic—A type in which the forms slant to the right

Justify—To set a line to a desired measure

Leading—The spacing between lines (measured in points)

Letterspacing—The space between the letters in a word

Lowercase letters (l.c.)—The small letters

Pica—A unit used to measure the length of a line of type. One pica (0.166″) consists of 12 points and six picas (72 pt.) equal one inch

Point—Used to measure the typesize—from the top of the ascender to the bottom of the descender plus space above and below to prevent the lines of type from touching. The point (0.1383″) is the basic unit of printer's measurement.

Ragged right , ragged left—Unjustifed type that is allowed to run to various line lengths

Roman—A type in which all the letters are upright.

Sans serif—A typeface without serifs

Serif—The short strokes that project from the ends of the main body strokes of a typeface

Typeface—A specific design for a type alphabet

Type family—All the styles and sizes of a given type

Word spacing—The spacing between words in a line

Uppercase letters (u.c. or c.)—The capital letters or caps

x-height—The height of the lowercase x in a given typeface

Three commonly used faces shown in various sizes.

Baskerville	Times Roman	Univers
9/10 Once upon a time once upon a time once upon a time once upon a time once upon a time once upon a time once upon	9/10 Once upon a time once upon a time once upon a time once upon a time once upon a time once upon a time once upon	9/10 Once upon a time on ce upon a time once upon a time once up on a time once upon a time once upon a time once upon a t
10/11 Once upon a time once upon a time once upon a time once upon a time once upon a time	10/11 Once upon a time on ce upon a time once upon a time once up on a time once upon a time once upon a	10/11 Once upon a time once upon a time once upon a time once upon a time once upon a time
11/12 Once upon a time once upon a time once upon a time once upon a time once upon a time once upon a time	11/12 Once upon a time o nce upon a time on ce upon a time onc e upon a time once upon a time once u pon a time once up	11/12 Once upon a time once upon a time once upon a time once upon a time once upon a time once upon a time

A showing of 18 pt. Souvenir Roman (the face used for this book).

abcdefghijklmnopqrstuvwxyz1234567890
ABCDEFGHIJKLMNOPQRSTUVWXYZ$

Trade
Gothic

Garamond

Century

**Cooper
Black**

Univers

Korinna

Gill Sans

Helvetica

Tiffany

Times Roman

Futura

even if the author agrees to the change, the cost of it should be borne by the publisher, not the author.

Once you have returned the galleys to the publisher, you will be pleased that your part of the job is done. You will also be impatient—even the most patient authors are—to see the illustrator finish his part of the work. This long lag between rough illustrations and finished is frustrating but unavoidable. Like the author, the illustrator is at the mercy of his Muse, and he can't be certain that the pictures will flow from his pen right on schedule. Some of the most enduring picture books take years to illustrate, and artists may also suffer from "blocks," as Blair Lent's eloquent account of his experience illustrating Arlene Mosel's Caldecott-winning *The Funny Little Woman* attests: "Ann Durrell [the editor of the book at Holt, Rinehart and Winston] sent me Arlene Mosel's spirited words during a dark time in my life, a time when I had trouble going on. Mrs. Mosel's comical adventures of the Funny Little Woman lifted my spirits. It is an important book for me because I finished it—after many years of not being happy with, or able to complete, any work at all. Ann Durrell was the right editor at the right time, and her friendship and involvement with the growth of the book was vital."

When the finished artwork arrives at the publishing house, it is first reviewed by the editor. If you have been cooperative up to this point, you can expect your editor to send you photocopies of the final drawings or invite you in to the office to go over the originals. The artwork itself, in color, is never sent to you through the mail, because its value is in the thousands or even tens of thousands of dollars.

After the editor and the author have reviewed the artwork for content, it is then passed on to the art director. The art director has to work with the color separator and the printer to ensure fidelity of the finished printing to the original paintings. This is a ticklish job.

The Finished Illustrations

There are three basic kinds of illustration, each with its own reproduction problems. The simplest kind is black-and-white artwork, which is being used more and more frequently as publishers become ever more cost-conscious. The simplest kind of black-and-white illustration is what you see on the comic pages of your daily paper—the line illustration. This line can be printed in any color—*Blueberries for Sal* was printed in a deep berry blue, *Make Way for Ducklings* in a warm brown—but it is printed in just one color. Sometimes an illustrator will introduce a delicate line that has to be shot for plate-making on film that can pick up every nuance and shading. This technique, called *fine line,* is an art director's nightmare, because in the process of picking up each subtle line of the drawing, the camera's objective eye also picks up every thumbprint, shadow, and smudge. There is no room for error, since the very delicacy of the rendering is what makes the fine-line illustration work.

Sometimes an illustrator wants to go a step further and create shadows and gradations of a single color. This is called *halftone*, or *continuous tone*, reproduction. (The best-known form of this kind of illustration is the photograph.) Illustrators like Dale Payson and Arnold Lobel can convey a whole spectrum in tones of a single color. The art director's concern with the halftone illustration is that it not become muddy. Some artists, like Joanne Scribner, prepare a halftone illustration, and then draw a holding line over that illustration to give form to the drawing.

In this cost-conscious era, the art of preseparated or hand-separated illustration has reached new heights. Suppose, like Robert Bright, you wrote a book about a red umbrella. If your publisher is concerned with expense, he may rule full-color paintings an extravagance; but that umbrella just has to be red. The enterprising illustrator will prepare a two-part drawing—a base drawing in black and white, and a superimposed drawing, called an *overlay*, in red. This approach can be used for two colors, as it is in *The Red Umbrella*, or for three, as in *Charlie Needs a Cloak*, or even four, as in *Little Fox Goes to the End of the World*. Many top illustrators, like Ray Cruz and Ron Barrett, actually prefer to separate their colors onto independent overlays, because they feel that this way they have more control over the colors. The most expensive and elaborate books feature *full color*, or *reflective*, illustrations. The colors in these illustrations are separated by a camera with a series of filters; there is a red plate, a blue plate, a yellow plate, and a black plate. In this process, the camera does the separation that an illustrator who separates his own work controls. The colors used in printing camera-separated work are called *process colors*, and they have been developed to produce the greatest fidelity to original artwork. The basic colors are not the red, yellow, and blue that you would expect but a garish magenta, a screaming yellow, and a vibrant turquoise blue called cyan. Combined with black, the fourth color, these strange hues reproduce the colors in the artist's palette quite closely.

While you pace the floor waiting for the illustration proofs to arrive, your editor, the art director, and the type designer are fussing over the camera copy for your book. The camera copy is the copy from which the printer shoots his film, and it must be perfect. Every line of type has to be straight; every illustration has to be positioned precisely so that no funny holes or inexplicable margins appear; and each proof of the color separation has to be painstakingly corrected so that there are no gaps—called *hickeys*—in the color, and that the canary yellow boots on page 7 are not lemon yellow on page 23.

The camera copy is mounted on large sheets of heavy white paper, usually with two facing pages mounted on the same piece of paper. When the printer receives the camera copy, sometimes called *mechanicals,* he makes negatives for each color used. Each negative represents a single color, so that the printer has to opaque the areas that are *not* to be printed in that color. Sensitized printing plates are then exposed to these negatives. The art director, the artist, and sometimes the editor correct printed proofs of each color, called *progressive proofs,* before the job goes on press. If the yellow is too strong, or the red too purple, these corrections are made before the job goes to press for the *edition run,* the actual printing of the book. Nonetheless, there are usually some small changes when the book is printed, as the printer adjusts the flow of ink, or straightens the paper or corrects color registration problems that arise while the job is on press.

The author's last chance to make emergency corrections is when the printer supplies the publisher with prints of the negatives from which the plates are made. These are usually *blue-line prints,* called *blues* in publishing slang, or *ozalid copies.* These prints give the editor and author a chance to make sure that the type and the pictures correspond exactly; they also give the art director and the artist a chance to see if the margins are correctly aligned, and if enough room has been left in the inside margin, or *gutter,* to allow for the sewing involved in children's book binding.

The Binding

This binding is designed to be durable. Dorothy White describes the abuse her daughter heaped on her beloved first book:

> It was a book fated to suffer every indignity that a child's physically expressed affection could devise—a book not only to be looked at, but licked, sat on, slept on, and at last torn into shreds. Solemn as parents are inclined to be over a firstborn, we argued gravely whether we should allow such destruction. Finally we decided, or, more accurately, drifted toward the belief, that the enjoyment of personal ownership was a fact of life more worth knowing than how to look after this or that.

This eminent librarian echoes the sentiments of most librarians, that a children's picture book should be able to stand up to wear and tear, from not just one child but many. For this reason, children's picture book publishers spend a great deal of time and money on binding children's books so that they are at once attractive and sturdy. The hardcover editions that are found on library shelves have a *reinforced binding.*

In the first step of this binding process, the pages are folded from the press sheet, and then gathered together in eight- or sixteen-page units, called *signatures.* Your editor may send you your book minus a cover, announcing that these are F&Gs, which is jargon for folded and gathered sheets.

The second step is called *casing-in.* The binding case is three pieces of heavy-weight cardboard, called *binder's board,* which the binding material wraps around. The front piece is called the *front plate,* the center sliver is called the *spine,* and the back plate is sometimes called the *back ad,* because it often carries advertising copy about the book, or about other books by the same author.

A piece of sturdy cambric cloth is inserted along the hinges of the case, between the spine and the front and back plates. The endpapers, usually solid-colored, sturdy paper, are inserted over the case, and the sheets are stitched in with side sewing around the signatures for maximum durability, or with Smyth sewing along the signatures for less durability but easier opening.

The Jacket and the Cover

Your book will have either a printed or a jacketed cover. The printed cover usually features a color illustration on the front, along with the title, the author's name, and the illustrator's name. The back cover features a short blurb describing the book's content or promoting another of your books, perhaps photos of you and the illustrator, the price, and the identification number, the ISBN (International Standard Book Number), which singles out your book from all the others published. The spine carries your name and the illustrator's, the title, and the name of the publisher.

If the cover is *not* printed, the book almost always has a jacket. The unprinted cover is usually made of a pretty colored cloth or cloth substitute (spun polyolefin, a nonwoven biteproof, waterproof, and tearproof material, is very popular), and features a stamped title on the spine and perhaps a simple line drawing on the front. The copy on the jacket is traditionally broken up this way: the front flap gives information about the book's content, including the price and the age group for which it is appropriate, and the back flap features biographical sketches of the author and the illustrator. The back ad of a jacket either includes illustration, continuing the theme of the front plate, or advertisements for other books by the same author and/or illustrator.

Jackets are printed with great care, on heavy paper with good reproduction quality. Once it is printed, the jacket is usually covered with a plastic laminate in order to protect it from scuffing, dirt, and smudging as it is handled.

The printed cover or the jacket is regarded as an indispensable advance selling tool by most publishing houses, so you can expect to see the jacket of your book before you see anything of its interior. This is frustrating to most artists, and to some authors, because they feel that the jacket can best be made to express the book in its totality *after* the book has been completed. But the "hurry up and wait" approach to publishing, in which editors and writers rush to complete their contribution so that the artist can take his time to make the illustrations right, requires that the jacket come first. The publisher needs some art to sell the book, and this is most often the jacket. If a publisher is investing $20,000 in a picture book, he will want to give the book every chance to sell in advance (more about this in the next chapter).

The production process is a complex one, involving many different people. It starts with you, as you write your manuscript, then moves to your editor, then to the type designer, then to the art director, then to the copyeditor, and then to the production department, from where it is sent on to the typesetter, printer, and binder. In this long chain of specialists, things are bound to go wrong. "There is no such thing as a perfect book," Frank Upjohn, the president of St. Martin's Press, used to tell me when I was a fledgling editor, and I refused to believe him. Five hundred books later, I'm convinced that he's right.

Glue seeps out of the binding case. A book that is prepared for Smyth sewing is side-sewn in order to meet a scheduled date. The soft blues of the artwork, so crucial to the mood of the story, are hard turquoise in the last few thousand copies printed because the pressman fell asleep on the job. A paste-up artist, moving a comma, places it upside down. What do you do when your book is the victim of production mistakes?

Some authors stew over it for months. They tell their friends in agonizing detail how this small imperfection has destroyed their otherwise flawless work of art. Others are too shy to say anything, for fear they will incur the editor's wrath and reduce their chances for subsequent acceptances. The happy medium is somewhere in between. Editors are used to gripes. Books are usually reprinted three or four times in their lifetime, so if you have specific reasonable suggestions to make about ways to improve the book—short of hiring a new artist, or changing the typeface—the editor will pass it on to the reprint editor. The reprint editor works with the production department to correct mistakes in already-printed books. Go ahead and write that furious letter to your editor—then throw it away and write him a calmer one that acquaints him with your disappointment without branding you a hysterical amateur. Enclose a simple memorandum that includes the title of your book and bears the heading *CORRECTIONS FOR REPRINTS*. The corrections should be accompanied by the appropriate page numbers. Sign it, and keep a copy for your files.

It is important to remember that you are examining the book more closely than any reader will. Mistakes that turn your stomach will most likely go unnoticed by your readers. I can't remember the last time I read a novel that didn't have a typographical error in it—I probably never have—but it has never kept me from enjoying and admiring what I am reading. The same is true of the picture book. One of my earliest traumas in book publishing was a perfect gem of a picture book that was cased into an upside-down cover. When the first copy came in we dismissed it as a fluke, but to our horror, the whole printing had been bound upside down. I marvel now that I lost sleep over it then, but I did—for days. A senior editor stopped by my office to admire the book. "But it's bound upside down!" I wailed. The editor, a down-to-earth New Englander, replied without a pause, "Don't worry. Most people will never notice, and the few who do will know enough to understand how easily something like this can happen."

It's good advice. As you become involved in children's picture book publishing, you will become an expert on printing, binding, typesetting, and art techniques. The more you know about these things, the more successfully you can write for this demanding form. But it's essential as you gather expertise to keep it in perspective, always remembering that your perfectionist eye is trained, through experience, to see small and even smaller details. Ludwig Bemelmans, the author of the great *Madeline* books, refused to look at his books once they were published. Maybe that wasn't as crazy as it seemed.

14

Promoting and Selling Your Book

It is a Sunday afternoon on New York's Upper West Side. In the rear of a children's bookstore called Eeyore's sits Karla Kuskin, author and illustrator of *Roar and More* and many other picture and poetry books for children, reading aloud to an audience of children ages four to eleven. She attracts not only the very young children who enjoy her poetry but also older ones who recall reading her picture books when they were younger—advancing age hasn't dampened their enthusiasm for an author whose work they love. Meanwhile, in the front of the store, the cashier is busy ringing up sales of her books that have been put on display to coincide with her appearance. "The things children always want to know," Kuskin says, "are how old you are and how much money you make. They are very enterprising about finding out. One minute they will ask me, How old were you when you wrote this book? and a few minutes later they will ask how long ago I wrote it."

Like many established picture book authors, Kuskin finds that personal appearances do more to sell books than any advertising campaign. Joel Fram, the owner of Eeyore's, plans similar gatherings at his store most Sundays, because he too finds that this is what sells books.

Fram is typical of the professional who works with children's picture books. Like librarians and teachers, he accepts the long hours and low pay because he loves and believes in children's books. His bookstore, which opened on a side street several years ago, is now flourishing on Broadway, with a new branch opening on the East Side. Like all professionals in the field, he is familiar with the old classics and constantly on the lookout for new favorites.

Although Fram has been successful in his bookstore, most children's books are sold to schools and libraries. The selection process is monitored by trained librarians and teachers, experts who have studied children's literature in college and in graduate school. They are familiar with the standard favorites, and judge new titles by the highest standards and the most scrupulous selection process. In most library systems, "I like this book" is not reason enough for a purchase. Usually a librarian or teacher is called upon to justify her choice with favorable supporting reviews.

This arduous reviewing process makes the marketing of children's books different, from the beginning, from that of other books. Adult books are sold "in advance," that is, before the book is actually published. Children's books sell slowly when they are first released. Sales rise markedly at the end of the first year, when all the reviews have been published, and continue steadily though not as spectacularly through the life of the book. This long wait for a book to hit its stride is the frustrating characteristic of children's book marketing.

"Wait." "Be patient." These are the admonitions that the writer is likely to hear from his editor when he asks nervously, "How is my book doing?" Here is a rough chronology of the way a children's book is sold:

First Steps

As soon as your book is put under contract with a publisher, the sales effort begins. Here's another facet of the vital importance of your relationship with your editor. If there's a real bond of friendship, you've got an edge—he's just bound to have that little bit of extra fondness for your book, and he will communicate that enthusiasm to the sales and marketing staff. Every season, one or two or three lucky books on a publisher's list will become general favorites throughout the publishing house. A wave of enthusiasm starts with the editor and his staff, and sweeps through the house. Pretty soon everyone working for the publisher is talking about—you hope—Your Book. From the chairman of the board to the mailroom clerk, you've got them on your side. This kind of in-house enthusiasm is an invaluable secret weapon, as anyone who's worked in publishing will tell you, because it communicates itself to the most hardened salesmen. And it originates with the editor.

The first concrete step in the process is the circulation through the office of an info sheet called something like "About the Book" or "The Editor Says." This sheet will emphasize the book's sales points, the distinguishing characteristics that will draw readers to your book over another book. For instance, the sales points for June Goldsborough's *What's in the Woods?*, an alphabet book that introduces the animals of the Northeast woods in a storybook setting, are: (1) an alphabet book (*always* in demand); (2) authentic research to ensure accuracy (a draw for nature buffs); (3) realistic illustrations (suitable to the nonfiction subject and setting); (4) a plot that is a low-key mystery (mysteries, posing an unanswered question, always draw the reader to the end to find the answer). The sales representatives who will ultimately be selling the book study these sales points with the same fervor as a baseball fan boning up on batting averages, because these characteristics help him distinguish your book from the thousands of others that are being sold at the same time.

You can help your book at this stage by examining your manuscript carefully for sales features that set it apart from the crowd. Since you know the manuscript better than anyone else, you will be able to point out surprising and useful details that make it special. Write these items down—don't be shy!—and send them to your editor. This will get your book off to a running start.

The Jacket

The second step in the selling of a book is the preparation of the jacket. As I noted in the last chapter, the jacket is printed far in advance of the book. Many illustrators prepare the jacket illustration as soon as they have finished the rough dummy for the book, so that the sale representatives will have something to show prospective customers. This advance jacket is called a proof, and various people's reactions to it will often result in modifications. The green of the background may not be eye-catching enough, the author's name may be too small; sometimes even the title is changed.

Here again, the author can help the publisher promote the book by providing thoughtful information about himself and what he has written to be used in creating the jacket copy.

The copy on the front flap of the jacket describes the book's content. The purpose of this copy is to hook a reader, so the emphasis is put on the theme of the book without divulging the resolution of the plot. Imagine that you are having lunch with a child, and in that quiet time after lunch, the two of you are going to share your story. "I know a good book," you are saying, "about a little girl who is lost in the jungle and meets a tiger." "And what happens then?" the child asks eagerly. "We'll have to read the book and see," you say. This is the approach of front flap copy. Characters and setting should be played up, whereas the mechanics of the plot should be played down. If the book is humorous or a tearjerker, this should be mentioned without giving away *how* the writer creates laughter or tears.

The back flap is no less important. Your contribution starts with a photograph of yourself. Keep that glamorous standard studio shot for your definitive study of eighteenth-century English country homes. Children want to see what you look like, to find out something about you as a person, and a picture can truly be worth a thousand words in realizing this goal. A casual snapshot, a picture of you with your own children, even a picture of yourself as a child—all are more appealing to young tastes than a mug shot.

If you have written a book about ships, you might want to send in a picture of yourself on the water; if you have written a book set in the mountains, you might want to include a picture of yourself in full hiking regalia. Bernard Most created a wonderful picture book for very young children called *Turn Over.* "Why is Cindy crying?" the text asks about a tearful little girl. "Turn over," the text tells the reader. "Cindy is crying because she slipped on her skates and ripped her pants!" This front view/back view picture book theme is carried out in the author's picture, which features Most's head, rear view, at the beginning of the biography, and a smiling front view (turned over) at the end of the biography. Charles Keller included a caricature of himself drawn by cartoonist-illustrator F.A. Fitzgerald, who illustrated Keller's *Daffynitions.* The theme of the book was carried through to the author and artist pictures.

The text for the back flap copy calls for a similar lighthearted approach. Your fellow alums of Penn State may be thrilled to recognize you as member of the Class of '62, but the young reader is going to be far more interested in what you did when you were a kid and what you do when you aren't writing. Are you an expert kite flyer? Do you like to bake cookies? Can you recite the RBI totals for every White Sox player since 1970? These are matters of primary concern for young readers. And as any picture book writer's fan mail attests, kids are more eager than any other group of readers to know about their authors as people.

In the preparation of advertising copy, modesty is the writer's enemy. Your publisher will be advertising your book in professional journals for teachers and librarians as well as your local paper—and good copy will call attention to your book. Don't worry—if you have overstated your strengths and sound far more interesting than any writer could possibly be, your editor is an expert at paring down the hyperbole. But pertinent—even outrageous—points about yourself and your book give the editor and the marketing staff the "something to work with" that a simple statement of where you were born, where you went to school, and what your occupation is leave out.

Blowing Your Own Horn

Your editor will be responsible for presenting your book at the sales conference, where the in-house marketing staff gets together with the field sales representatives to discuss new titles and pull together information that will help the field representatives sell the new books. The presentation your editor makes usually consists of information about the book and the person who wrote it, the sales points mentioned above, and the unveiling of the jacket proof. Sometimes with picture books, samples of the artwork beyond the cover are provided to give the sales people a sense of what the final book will look like. Your editor works hard at the sales conference. With butterflies in his stomach, he faces the ho-hum looks on the sales reps' faces. Editors make surprising and sometimes funny efforts to have *your* book remembered, whether it is passing around cookies from a cookbook, doing cartwheels to dramatize an exercise book, or suddenly bawling like a calf to act out an alphabet book on a farm theme.

After the sales meeting, the sales representative takes the jacket to various customers—book wholesalers like Baker and Taylor, which supply libraries with a central ordering source, the buyers for the large chains like Walden and B. Dalton, which feature some (but by no means all) new children's books, and large library systems and small children's bookstores where the expert customers like to know what's coming up.

Despite these intensive sales efforts, it's very common for a writer to fail to find his book in his local bookstore. Usually the author puts the blame on the publisher, faulting his sales coverage, but the truth is, nobody is to blame. The publisher's representative shows the book to the local bookstore, touting the writer as a local author. But the local bookstore usually can't afford to stock the author's books unless there is some concrete plan to actually sell those books. This is where the author's ingenuity comes in. He may sneak around town like Mata Hari asking for his book at *every* store, and rounding up his friends to follow suit. A friend of mine has a devoted aunt who is expert at re-arranging the books in a store so that his books are prominently dis-played—and she does this while pretending to browse.

As soon as you receive your jacket proof, write your local book-store owner a note, or stop by with a copy of the proof, and ask him to stock your book. Suggest an autographing party or a display. If you have written a story about a rabbit, suggest an Eastertime promotion with a live rabbit. If you have written a story about a child in a pioneer family, suggest a demonstration of patchwork quilt making to draw crowds to the bookstore. If you have written a story about a goose who loves ice cream, suggest renting an ice-cream freezer and selling cones on the sidewalk outside the store. Sure, these ideas are farfetched, maybe corny, but they start people thinking about tie-ins that can be used to promote your book. With a tie-in, the bookstore owner is a lot more likely to order your book.

"What's new?" customers ask Vicky Swingell, manager of The Owl and the Pussycat Bookstore in Lexington, Kentucky. "For the pic-

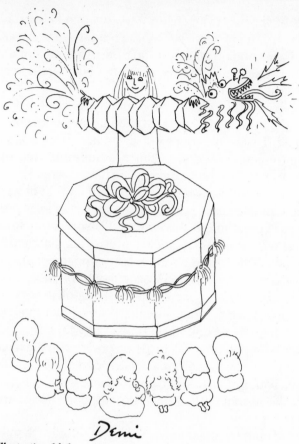

Illustration 14-1.

In order to promote her many books based on oriental themes, author/artist Demi entertains groups of children in bookstores, museums and schools with her Chinese Sunday box, an old New England tradition from the days of the China trade, in which she keeps Chinese toys and copies of her picture books for reading aloud.

ture book age," Swingell maintains, "the assumption is that the family already has the classics, especially if there are older children in the family. People are looking for new books, exciting books."

Your local library is another possible outlet for promoting your book. Offer your services for a story hour, reading your book. Have an autograph party at the library with the proceeds of the sale going to a fund for the children's room. Let your librarian know that you are available to speak about your book to library groups and teachers' associations. Librarians are as interested as anyone else in what the author has to say.

Chalk talks, where a writer sketches characters on a blackboard, and demonstrations, in which the process of bookmaking is elaborated, are popular in classrooms. You can spend a single afternoon in a school and reach hundreds of children. The children will want to know such crazy things as how rich you are, what books you read when you were in second grade, and what you do when you go to New York. Your answers will spark their interest in your book, no matter how far the conversation strays from the book itself.

There are many ways to drum up support for your book before it is published. Writers' groups will like to listen to your war stories about how you got published. Teachers' groups will like to hear what you try to achieve in writing for young children. Church groups and civic organizations will be interested in the subject area you have written about, especially if it is of local interest. As soon as you have the proof of your book jacket in hand, start talking up your book to interested local professionals and groups. Forget about the Johnny Carson show: local promotion is the best way to get your book started. Talk, talk, talk!

When your book arrives from your publisher, the temptation is to feel that you have done your job. No instinct could be more mistaken: your work is just beginning. Send a copy of the book to your local newspaper, even if it is just a penny shopper, with a letter that describes your connection to the neighborhood. Send copies, along with a press release, which your publisher will help you prepare, to the town where you went to high school, the college you attended, the university where you have taken writing courses. The press release will emphasize your affiliation with the institution that will publicize your book, and your book will speak for itself.

If you know the name of anyone who can give your book publicity, tell your editor. Your book itself is its own best advertisement. Publishers are usually very generous about sending copies to book reviewers, reporters, and media specialists. It is not unusual for a publisher to send out 500 copies to various reviewers.

Now is the time for you to follow up on the visits you have made to bookstores, schools, and libraries. Thanks to your advance warning of the book's publication, they will be ready to make a space to promote your book. If anyone seems to be disappointed with your book and thus unwilling to promote it, give him an argument! Point out its strengths, explain its weaknesses, but never accept a personal criticism of your book as a reason not to promote it. If a reporter has negative opinions about your writing, but wants to do an article anyway, let him write. Even adverse publicity is better than none.

Reviews and Reviewers

Reviewers, like all writers, write to be read. Reviewers have learned that the glowing review is sometimes a pleasure to read, but—alas!—a vitriolic review is often more fun. Since reviewers count on their readership for their jobs, they are sometimes more than willing to write a spicy, unfavorable review. The writer has to respect the reviewer's craft and to swallow the bad review with a grain of salt. This is sometimes difficult to the point of impossibility. Reviewers can criticize a book because it is not the book the reviewer would have written. Reviewers can overlook the fact that the author is writing for three- and four-year-olds and point out information that could have been included if the book had been intended for older children. Reviewers can compare the writer's output to the most incongruous model, but never mind—any space in the newspaper or magazine is better than no mention at all. At least people know your book exists.

The first review of your book that you will see will be in *Kirkus Reviews*. This esteemed semimonthly publication is written for professional librarians who are selecting books for their collections. These librarians see thousands of books every year, and they welcome *Kirkus*'s thoughtful assessment of almost everything new. *Kirkus* is a serious publication and provides a genuine service to its readers: the prose is entertaining without fail, with only the author as victim. The fact that its reviews are overwhelmingly negative need give a new author only a passing pang. Since *Kirkus* is the review of record, its reviews matter a great deal, but it's important to understand that *Kirkus* is more market-conscious than its competitors at *School Library Journal* or *Publishers Weekly*. *Kirkus* wants to be readable, and negative reviews are always more interesting and readable than positive ones. But *Kirkus* is just one review medium: a *Kirkus* star for excellence is no guarantee that other periodicals will find your book delightful.

The next review that you encounter will be in the *School Library Journal*. This is a centrally important review since librarians and teachers have come to count on *SLJ*, as it is affectionately known, to give them the lowdown on new titles. Unlike *Kirkus*, which has a staff of professional reviewers, *SLJ* counts on librarians, whose only payment is the books themselves. The reviews reflect regional prejudice, personal taste, and professional training, pluses or minuses depending on what the review says. Since *SLJ* reviewers are not paid, the reviews are sometimes slow in coming—you may have to wait up to two years! For established authors the process is much faster. The editors of *SLJ* are well aware of the prejudice this reflects and try to counteract it by speeding up the reviewing process for newer authors.

If you are lucky enough to catch the eye of the editors at *Horn Book, Booklist, Publishers Weekly,* or the *Bulletin of the Center for Children's Books,* your book is far ahead. Unlike *Kirkus* and *SLJ*, these periodicals are limited to the offerings they think are likely to attract the most notice, or the ones that they want to especially recommend. Nothing can sway these professionals. They judge the book itself, nothing more, nothing less. A review in either *Horn Book* or *Booklist* constitutes a recommendation. A review of a book in *Publishers Weekly,* positive or negative, brings it to the attention of book buyers in the stores. Reviewer Jean Mercier of *Publishers Weekly* maintains that there are so many books worth reviewing that she can't fulfill the magazine's promise that books are reviewed before they are published, yet her sensitive evaluations are always noticed.

As important as these reviews are to establishing your book, they are not the end-all for a picture book writer. Although you will find that your book is usually reviewed within the first two years of its publication, there is no reason it can't continue to receive attention as it grows older. Successful picture book writers promote their previous books with each new book. They never stop selling what they have had published. Their determination and pride in the finished book is what sells books—bookstore owners, librarians, teachers, parents, older children, sisters and cousins and aunts all catch the contagious enthusiasm for the book, no matter how long it's been around, and pass it on. Word of mouth, starting with *your* word, is what sells books.

15

A Writer's Survival Kit

Books are made to protect writing, good writing, from oblivion. A book can be forever, but if you don't make sure it lasts, who will?

You have done the essential parts. Your topic is well researched, the book is sensitively written, and you have chosen the right publisher for it.

Now is the time to protect your job well done. By expecting the unexpected, as this chapter outlines, you can prepare for the possibility that your book won't catch on right away but will enjoy popularity later. Although some of the information here is highly technical, it's worth plowing through because it may prove to be surprisingly useful. Children's paperbacks are one of the fastest-growing areas of the publishing industry, and the opportunities for finding a home there for your out-of-print picture book have never been better.

Protect Your Rights

When a publisher refuses to offer you a contract unless he can purchase all rights outright, negotiate. Your story is probably worth far less to him than it is to you. If a publisher wants to purchase a story outright, I always advise a writer to accept a lower fee and grant to the publisher only one-time or limited rights. In this way, the publisher saves money by paying you less, and you make money because you will be sure that the story can be marketed in other ways. A story sold outright to a publisher often languishes in the publisher's archives when an enterprising author could be selling and reselling it.

Margery Williams's *The Velveteen Rabbit,* written fifty years ago, has never gone out of print. Recently it has enjoyed a new popularity, largely with college students. It is available now in three paperback editions. No one could have predicted that this would be the one book of its year and decade that would enjoy such an enormous resurgence of popularity. Your book may be a big hit the year it is written, but it is far more typical for children's books to catch on more slowly, sometimes years after they have been published. What you must be alert to is the chance that your book will find a new audience years after it has gone out of print. This possibility is not so farfetched as many authors believe, and with careful planning you can prepare for it.

Three Safeguards for Your Book

There are three precautions you should plan for, from the moment you sign the contract: (1) that you have an adequate supply of books, even once your book is out of print; (2) that you have the rights to reprint the book once it has gone out of print; and (3) that you have the materials you need to manufacture a new edition of the book. All of these points are covered in your contract. The publisher will supply you with a certain number of free copies of the book—usually ten—and will allow you to purchase additional copies at a discount, usually 40 percent off the list price. Second, your contract should stipulate a procedure for the reversion of the rights to you once the publisher is no longer actively selling the book.

Third, your contract will contain a manufacturing-materials clause which will give you the choice of purchasing—at a bargain price—the films from which your book is printed. These films are bulky and even at bargain rates they are expensive, but they sometimes make a sound investment.

Why am I reading this technical nonsense? you ask. *My* book is not going out of print.

The statistics suggest otherwise. In the good old days, children's books had an average life of twenty years and it was always easy for the author to purchase copies of his books as he needed them. The mechanics of sales through libraries made it possible for publishers to order large first printings that would ensure that the author could get a copy of his book by phoning the publisher any time. Today, things are different. The average (and that's all it is—an average) life of a children's picture book is five years. If it's in print for less than that, you are entitled to be disappointed; for more, you can be very proud.

Keeping a Supply of Books

First of all, you must follow agent Julian Bach's advice and *buy your book.* Buy eighty copies, a hundred, even five hundred. Don't keep them in your living room where you will be tempted to give them away. When they arrive, check that the copies are indeed copies of your book, and that they have no physical defects, then store them in an out-of-the-way, cool, dry place. When Christmas comes and you are short on presents, stay away from that box. It is your insurance. Those copies of your book should be used for professional reasons only. As samples of your previously published work when you are trying to sell a new manuscript, as thank-yous—autographed for a re-

porter who has mentioned your book or for a reviewer who has reviewed it sensitively—and for general goodwill, such as donation to a
local book fair or a newly opened library, they will be invaluable.

When your supply of books dwindles down to a half-dozen, you
should begin to be very careful. Not even your new mother-in-law is
eligible for a copy when your supply is this short. It is hard to imagine
when you think of ten thousand copies of your book sitting in the
publisher's warehouse that there will come a time when not a single
copy of the book is available. And you will *always* need copies of the
book.

When Dorothy Wisbeski and Edna Miller wrote and illustrated
Picaro: The Story of a Pet Otter, they had no way of knowing that the
book would be available for only a year. The publisher went out of the
children's book business, the artwork disappeared (as it sometimes
will), and the author and the artist had given all their copies of the book
away—all except one file copy, which they guarded jealously. This file
copy became the shooting copy for the paperback edition of the book
eleven years later. If it had not been for that sole copy, the book would
have gone out of existence.

OOS and OOP

To protect your book, begin by understanding what *in print*
means. When a book is printed, it's in print. It stays in print as long as it's
physically available. For instance, when *George the Babysitter* was
printed, Prentice-Hall, its publisher, ordered 8,000 copies to be printed
and bound. Before it was actually in print, the sales people took orders
for the book from bookstores. As soon as the book was physically
available, it was shipped to bookstores. As soon as the bookstores sold
their initial supply of *George the Babysitter,* they could order new
copies from the publisher, because *George the Babysitter* was in print.

The book sold better than Prentice-Hall expected it to. The supply of printed copies ran short of the demand. There was a lag between
the first printing and the second. The book was then declared *out of
stock.* That meant that every time a bookstore ordered a copy of
George the Babysitter, the order came back with a notation, OOS, with
a date indicated for the book to be back in stock, or in print. Going out
of stock is not a good thing for a book, but it isn't the end of the world. If
a book is out of stock, the bookseller may suggest a substitute on the
same subject to his customer, and you will lose a sale. (Most children's
books are purchased for special occasions—the arrival of a baby sister,
graduation from nursery school, birthdays and Christmas—so most
picture book customers are unwilling to wait.) Or, if the customer wants
your book—and no other will do—the bookseller will tell him to return
to the store after a certain date to pick the book up.

Most publishers have a provision in their contracts that they will not let a book stay out of stock for more than six months. If a book is out of stock for six months, the author usually has the same rights as the author whose book is out of print.

What is *out of print?* A book is out of print when no new printing is planned to replenish the exhausted supply. If the book is not selling well at all, the book may be allowed to "go out of print." This means that the publisher will continue to sell the book, but does not plan to reprint it. This is not information that the publisher shares with the author.

To keep track of your book's print history, you need to know how to read a royalty statement. If no sales are made during a six-month royalty period, inquire, because your book is probably OOS.

When your book goes out of stock, make a note of the date when you first heard about its being unavailable. Some writers order a few copies every three months, just to be sure the book is still available. Others ask their editors how many copies are to be printed in the first printing (this information is often decided at the last minute, so be patient) and keep a running tally of copies sold by checking their royalty statements.

Be sure that your royalty statement indicates how many copies are sent to reviewers and media for no charge as well as how many copies have actually been sold, if you are using this second method of keeping track. If this information is missing, ask your editor for it.

How to Read Your Royalty Statement

A royalty statement can be confusing. One area of confusion is the advance. Many authors overlook the advance payment when they read their royalty statement and see that books have been sold, royalties have been earned, but no check is enclosed. The income from book sales is deducted from the advance. With a large advance it can be three or four royalty periods before it is "earned back." Until it is earned, a minus amount is shown under "balance due." Once you have earned back your advance, your balance should stop being a negative amount.

It is also important to remember that royalties are paid at several different rates (which are listed in your contract) according to the type of sale the publisher has made. The royalty on the hardcover edition, for example, is different from that paid on the paperback. In addition to book sale income the royalty statement reflects sales of subsidiary rights. Most often these are lump sums which appear separately on your statement.

Returns are also shown on royalty statements. If your book sells many copies during early royalty periods, it is always possible that these copies will come back to the publisher. As Alfred Knopf once said of book returns, "gone today, here tomorrow." Careful reading of your royalty statement will clear up most questions; your editor can answer the rest. Remember, royalty statements are subject to error, so you should scrutinize them as carefully as you would a bank statement.

As soon as you hear that your book is out of stock, write a letter to your editor, requesting information about when a new printing is planned. Publishers run up against all kinds of unforeseen delays in planning reprints: the paper isn't available, the printer is overbooked, the films don't get to the printer in time. Again, it makes sense to be patient, but you want to be sure that the publisher honors the six-month grace period in your contract. If your book is out of stock, it will be unavailable to the public, and your fickle audience will substitute other picture books for yours. You can't afford this.

Suppose your book goes out of print. What do you do then? The first thing you do is write to your publisher citing the paragraph of your contract that applies to rights reversion. Phone calls won't do in these legal matters; everything must be done in writing, with file copies in case the follow-up is faulty.

Send the letter registered mail. It should go something like this:

Dear Publisher,

According to Clause _____ of my contract for _____ dated _____, rights to the book will revert to me upon my written request.
This letter constitutes a request for rights to revert to me for the title_____.
I look forward to hearing from you within _____ days, as stipulated in the contract.

Rights to Reprint the Book

A standard, and very fair, reversion clause will contain the following provisions: (1) the publisher will notify you three months before the book goes out of print; (2) the publisher will offer you the remaining stock, usually a minimum of fifty copies and a maximum of a thousand, at the manufacturing cost plus handling charges; (3) once the book is out of print, upon written notice from you, the publisher will return all rights to you; and (4) for a nominal price, usually half the cost of making the original films from which the printing plates are made, you can purchase the publisher's manufacturing materials so that you can manufacture the book yourself.

Purchasing the Films

When the publisher informs you that the rights have reverted to you, write to him again and ask him what manufacturing materials are available to you and at what price. With a picture book, the purchase of the films (some publishers follow the archaic practice of calling them "plates") by an author is complicated somewhat by the fact that artwork and text appear on the same page together. It is simple enough, however, for the printer to cut the text film apart from the illustration film. If you know the artist, or if your editor is willing to give you the artist's name and address, it is possible that the two of you can collaborate—with or without an agent—in the purchase of films, and try to resell the book together.

Once you know the price and a full and accurate manufacturing description (such as "right reading, emulsion side down, negatives"), you will want to call the local printer and find out what kind of storage is required for this kind of film. Usually the same cool, dry place where you store your books is sufficient protection for printing materials.

Having added up the price of the materials and how much the storage will cost in terms of space as well as price, you will want to consider seriously the pros and cons of buying them. True, they don't make very attractive wall hangings, but it's also true that if you don't purchase them now, you won't be able to purchase them at a bargain rate later. Reshooting the book to make new films can be prohibitively expensive. So follow your instincts. If you love the book, and feel that the writing is just right and the typography is just the way you like it, it makes good economic and aesthetic sense to purchase the films. If the illustrations were a disappointment, the typography old-fashioned, and the overall look one that you would like to see disappear with time, it makes sense to bypass the opportunity to buy the films.

Once you have the films in hand, you are in a position to present your book to publishers for reprint. The reprint package should contain the same elements as the original submission to the publisher: a covering letter, a résumé, and a copy of manuscript (in its pristine original form), plus a copy of the finished book. In addition, you may want to provide information about the artist (a résumé, and even a second covering letter or inclusion of the artist's comments in your covering letter) and copies of key reviews.

The films will make it easier for the publisher to accept your book because they will lower his costs of getting the book into print. The reviews will help him accept the book because he can judge from them how well the book was originally received.

When should you submit your out-of-print book? Many writers

wait until their topic becomes topical again. A book on solar energy, written fifteen years ago when the subject was brand-new, may be ready for a reprint now that the subject is in the headlines again. On the other hand, a story about a black girl and a white girl making friends, so timely twenty years ago, may need a little more time to come into fashion again now that interracial friendships are common enough not to need the reinforcement of another book example.

If it is the illustrations that appear outdated, the publisher will find an artist to provide new ones. This was the case with Charlotte Zolotow's *One Step, Two* ... which was reissued with new illustrations after being out of print (see illustrations 15-1 and 15-2).

Just because your book is out of print is no reason to consider it dead. If you plan carefully, an out-of-print book becomes another hot property, another chance at success and sales.

Illustrations 15-1 and 15-2.

Charlotte Zolotow's One Step, Two..., *like any good picture book manuscript, lends itself to different interpretations. The original illustrations by Roger Duvoisin reflect the values and outlook of the post-war era, when the book was first published; Cindy Wheeler lends a contemporary air to the illustrations in this endearing reissue of a classic picture book.*

16

The Second Book— and Beyond

Years after the publication of their first book, writers who have gone on to write scores more can still tell you all about it. For Charlotte Zolotow, it was, well, a storybook experience. Zolotow, whose inspired creative writing had been drawing attention from the time she was in elementary school, was working as a secretary to Ursula Nordstrom, the great children's editor at Harper & Row (then Harper & Brothers). Margaret Wise Brown was publishing with Harper's at that time, and Zolotow thought that Brown might be interested in writing a book for the Harper list about a city park. Nordstrom agreed it was an excellent suggestion, and encouraged Zolotow to jot down her ideas. When Zolotow showed Nordstrom her outline for the book, Nordstrom suggested she flesh it out. Zolotow expanded the proposal and passed it on to Nordstrom, thinking Nordstrom would then pass it on to Brown. Instead, Nordstrom brought the proposal back to Zolotow, saying, "Congratulations. You have just written your first picture book."

"It only happens that way once!" says Zolotow with a grin. *The Park Book,* with illustrations by H.A. Rey, is still thriving after more than thirty-five years in print.

Guy Billout got his start in print when publisher Harlin Quist, for whom Billout had done some illustrations, asked him if he had ever thought of writing his own story. For Billout, this was a dream come true. He created a storybook without words about what happens while a man waits for a bus. After he had finished the book, he had an altercation with Quist about a contractual matter. Sure he would find another publisher, Billout withdrew the book and began to make the rounds, only to find that every editor wanted changes to suit himself. Finally one publisher nearly accepted the book—"with just a few little changes." Disheartened, Billout accepted Harlin Quist's original offer. Published as *Number 24,* the book has sold a quarter of a million copies in exactly the form he wrote it.

Both Billout and Zolotow went on after these initial successes to write other books. Zolotow, the creator of the "mood" book for very young children, has concentrated on that genre, perfecting her prose and exploring such subjects as relationships with parents, experiences of the senses, and exploration of the emotions. Billout, whose first story won him international acclaim, has branched out into nonfiction, creating beginning books with a personal touch on engineering, transportation, and mythology.

What determines a picture book writer's direction? Why did these writers make the decisions they did to pursue new directions, or to concentrate on a single subject area?

Have You Begun a Series?

The first book is a hard act to follow. If a book is very successful, the obvious next step is a sequel. Children of the picture book age look for further adventures about their heroes by favorite authors, just as adults clamor for more Victoria Holts and John D. MacDonalds. Series books—from Russell Hoban's *Frances* to James Marshall's *George and Martha* to Edna Miller's *Mousekin*—are sure of an audience. But writers sometimes find confinement to a series stultifying. Hoban, Marshall, and Miller are typical in choosing to alternate series books with individual titles, such as *Dinner at Alberta's, Yummers!,* and *Pebbles.* Before he begins a sequel of any sort—especially a "series" sequel—the writer who has sold a picture book should examine his interests and his career plans carefully. The first step is to consider whether you really want to keep writing for the picture book age. The picture book writer is one of the most personal of writers, and the degree of involvement he brings to his books is going to be a large component of his success. "I write and I draw," says Jan Adkins, author of *Art and Industry of Sand Castles* and other imaginative nonfiction works, "but what I really do is learn. I learn about something that interests me, something I can find wonder in, and I try to explain it clearly without losing that wonder. I'm a professional looker and learner and a catcher in the rye by vocation." The most important thing a picture book writer learns about is himself. The safest, and most exciting, course for your second book and beyond is the one that is truest to your interests and your sense of wonder.

As Margaret Mahy, the author of twenty books for young children, so aptly observes, "There are certain sorts of stories and certain uses of language which seem most appropriate in stories intended for children. It is almost as if there are certain images left over, insufficiently assimilated in one's own childhood. All stories, even the simplest ones, seem to be little pieces of biography, even if what one is recounting is only one's childhood games and dreams." If you do want to write for the picture book age, and are comfortable conjuring up circumstances, conversations, and characters that ring true with young readers, you are right in wanting to attempt a second book.

Inspiration is the next step. Kathryn Ernst, who has written both fiction (*Owl's New Cards; Danny and His Thumb*) and nonfiction (*Indians*) for the picture book age, found that as her inspiration grew up, her writing interests shifted. "The only reason I wrote children's picture books was because of my stepchildren. Not that I wrote books *for* them. Or that I used their lives and experiences as subject matter. Rather, talking with, thinking with them, watching them, being interested in how they thought about and felt about themselves and the world made me remember what it was like as a child."

This inspiration to stay in touch with the child in yourself is an ingredient that most writers for this age find essential. "I write for the child in me," Charlotte Zolotow says. Some people don't need outside inspiration to become attuned to this child, while others do. Some writers find that as their children grow up, grandchildren inspire further stories. Others, like Ezra Jack Keats, find that the inspiration is renewed and replenished within themselves. "I'm an ex-kid," the Caldecott-winning author-illustrator says. "We all have within us the whole record of our childhood. What I do is address the child within myself. And try to be as honest as possible and then hope for the best."

Hoping for the best can be aided by sound analysis and critical judgment. When Tomie de Paola wrote the story of a shepherd who made his own cloak, in *Charlie Needs a Cloak,* a flood of mail came in from appreciative readers suggesting sequels. His artist's instinct warned him against the idea. The first book had been an inspiration, and any follow-up titles would be pale in comparison. "I realized the absurdity of a sequel when a friend jokingly suggested that I write a book called *Charlie Makes a Drink*," de Paola laughs.

Subject matter is just one of the areas a second-round writer has to consider. A careful study of the book you have published can give you distance to see your own strengths and weaknesses. Is it your character that shines, as *Lyle, Lyle, Crocodile* does, or is it the mode of the storytelling, as in *Freight Train?* Is your sense of place your strength, as Robert McCloskey's is in his books, or is it the masterful weaving of various plot elements, as Don Freeman's is? The answers to these questions will guide you in planning a sequel and a sequence for your writing career.

With your first publication, you have made a mark, perhaps one that seems nearly imperceptible, but a mark nonetheless, on your audience. Somebody, and maybe many bodies, is going to ask for "another book by the person who wrote_____." If you feel that you have stumbled into a successful book by accident, and worry about how you are going to produce an encore, try to imagine yourself twenty years from now. What books would you like to see in your picture book bibliography? Make a list! Then consider which title would be the easiest for you to work on at the moment. For there will come a day when you will be associated with a list of books that define you to your public. Readers who never meet you will get to know you, and to feel they know you intimately, through your books. That's why integrity is such an important key to planning each book you write.

Do You Need an Alias?

Sometimes this leads to difficult decisions. Pseudonyms are frowned on by publishers who are eager to capitalize on your name, but they provide an invaluable safety valve for authors who are unhappy with the way the text has been changed. Early in her career, when Charlotte Zolotow wrote a book that was changed heavily in the editing, she made the difficult decision of using a nom de plume to protect her reputation as an original and unique writer. Some writers are better known for their pseudonyms than they are for the books they write under their own names.

Pseudonyms also benefit the prolific writer who doesn't want to risk having his craft dismissed by librarians and reviewers put off by a flood of books written in a short period. Nonwriters sometimes have a view of writing that seems odd to a writer: many reviewers seem to think that a writer enjoys a finite amount of inspiration in a lifetime and to produce too much over a short period of time spreads that inspiration thin. As a result, they are quick to see flaws in the work of a writer they consider overprolific. Writers know that inspiration is an uneven road, with some stretches producing lots of good ideas that lead to books, others leading nowhere. There's no "right" level of output.

Nonetheless, library budgets are limited, and it's only sensible for the writer to keep new books to a reasonable maximum. For most writers, this is three books a year. Libraries can afford to buy three new books by a given writer, provided they meet the libraries' standards, but more than that is stretching it. Many libraries pride themselves on complete collections of writers' works, but they are likely to give up if you produce too many too fast.

So the pseudonym is one way around the glut problem. Another solution is to write different kinds of books for different publishers. Demi, for instance, writes very simple stories for two- and three-year-olds for Random House, puzzle books for Doubleday, and Oriental folktales for Prentice-Hall, and saves her unexpected ideas for Holt, Rinehart and Winston. Tomie de Paola writes concept books for Holiday House, retold tales for Harcourt Brace Jovanovich, and humorous stories for Putnam's. Each publisher is working with a different aspect of the writer's talent and personality, so that librarians don't feel that they are working with a "book factory" but rather with a fascinating and multifaceted author. The diversity becomes a plus rather than a minus.

Many writers feel they should follow their publishers' advice, and write, almost as if they were on assignment, what their editors suggest. Sometimes this is a sensible policy. The arguments for sticking with a single publisher are many, and sound. Your editor knows you and understands your strengths, and you have already thrashed out a good working relationship. Your name is familiar to the sales representatives, and they will have an easier time pitching your books if they have more than one title to sell. The publisher will be better able to promote your books if he can spread the costs over several titles, some stronger than others. Different publishers reach different markets, however, and different editors can inspire a writer in different directions, so if you are ready to branch out in new directions, you might want to consider changing publishers. The exposure your books will get from several publishers reaches an ultimately wider audience than that of a single publisher.

Many writers feel that they need to publish as many titles as possible over a short space of time to impress their name on the book-buying public. While a barrage of reviews for different books does draw attention, there's no guarantee that the attention will be favorable. Far better to spread out the publication of your titles over a five-year period than to hope for overnight success. Overnight success does not occur in children's publishing.

It is in the longevity of a book, not sheer numbers of titles, that a picture book author finds his fame and fortune. James Daugherty is considered one of the towering geniuses of American picture book writing—on the basis of his perennial favorite, *Andy and the Lion.* Many fine writers for young children—Claire Huchet Bishop, Florence Parry Heide, Eleanor Estes—have written many books for different ages, but have confined their picture book offerings to a few beautifully written masterpieces. Yet they are as well loved and well known as many more prolific writers.

However you plan your picture book career, you will find satisfaction and challenge in it. Many children of picture book writers—Thatcher Hurd, Crescent Dragonwagon—have become picture book writers themselves.

Husband-and-wife teams, like Leonard and Ethel Kessler, Lenore and Erik Blegvad, and Aliki and Franz Brandenberg, find that writing and illustrating children's picture books together is a very satisfying career and lifestyle. There is something about the children's picture book—or should I say many things—that can occupy a lifetime of writing and growing through writing. The distillation and the purity that are required in writing for people who don't even know how to read yet challenge the most skilled and experienced writers. Nobody says it better than M.B. Goffstein: "The dignity and pleasure of being professional is to work and work in solitude—until it looks like you didn't have to work at all."

AFTERWORD: BREAKING THE RULES

This book is intended as a friendly guide to writing and selling picture books. In the service of that end, it contains many apparently cut-and-dried rules, regulations, and formulas; but don't let my words of wisdom mislead you into thinking that there is a single right way to write for young children. There is emphatically *not*. Every law I lay down has been broken, and a great part of the fun of writing for this age is deciding which rules to break and why it's important to break them to make your book effective.

Once you have written your story (or information or concept book) according to my recommendations, you may well find that in breaking some of the rules, you will strengthen your manuscript. It's important to remember that, once the rules are mastered, they can and often should be broken; but like a sculptor or painter or musician, in order to know how and when to break the rules, you have to learn them first.

In breaking the rules you'll find yourself in good company. I've told you, for instance, that every spread should contain at least a single word. But look at Randall Jarrell's *Snow White,* where the poet's translations alternate with breathtakingly beautiful, wordless full-color spreads of artwork by Nancy Elkholm Burkert. Or consider *Where the Wild Things Are.* Most of the pages contain text, but the book culminates in wildly comical and eerie wordless spreads that fill the page to bursting. Words here would be positively disruptive!

I also endorse brevity, but length is another highly controversial limitation. Mercer Mayer created a winning picture book in *A Boy, a Dog and a Frog* without including a word. And *Andy and the Lion,* surely one of the most successful picture books ever written, contains two and a half thirty-two-page signatures instead of the standard one. Furthermore, it is broken up into parts, heightening the suspense, and the humor, by deliberately interrupting the flow from page to page.

Many great picture books are far wordier than the paragraph maximums I've described. In *The Little Mermaid,* the text occupies full pages of type, set off with Dorothy Lathrop's haunting black-and-whites and luminous paintings on right-hand pages. If Hans Christian Andersen had followed my advice to the letter, his richly told tale would be reduced to gibberish! Another beautiful classic that contains a grown-up-sized text is *The Cat Who Went to Heaven,* by Elizabeth Coatsworth. Like *Andy and the Lion,* this book is broken into sections, in this case by short poems; and it too is long, with full pages of type interspersed with Lynd Ward's delicate brush drawings of animals. Ward breaks the words-on-every-page rule, too, with a moving double-page spread near the story's climax showing all the animals approaching Buddha, with the little cat Good Fortune at the end of the line. No child who grows up on this bittersweet Japanese tale ever forgets it.

The length limitations discussed in these pages may be too confining for nonfiction in particular. Holling C. Holling's *Minn of the Mississippi* and David Macaulay's *Cathedral* delight and inform children and adults alike by using the picture book format to convey specific information.

But are all these long books really for children? you ask. Certainly they are too long for the beginning reader, too long for a single sitting or a story-hour offering. But they are just right for many of the six-, seven-, and eight-year-olds who compose the upper age level of the picture book group, especially the advanced readers. It is also true that many great picture books have as strong an appeal to adults on one level as they do for children on another—*The Cat Who Went to Heaven* is a perfect example. There are also picture books that are virtually adult books in disguise. *The Giving Tree,* by Shel Silverstein, has been taken up by teenagers and college kids as the unrequited-love story that it is; at the same time, feminists glory in its woman-the-giver-man-the-taker theme, while ecologists shake their heads over its depiction of man as despoiler of nature. *Eloise* certainly makes its strongest appeal to urban adults, and adventurers of all ages are still pondering the treasure-hunt clues in Kit Williams's *Masquerade.*

Let's take a look at another "rule." In Chapter 5, I warn you against trying to combine fantasy and reality, because a blend that works is so difficult to achieve, and so rare. But when Bill Peet overlaps fantasy with the realism of the woods in *Merle, the High-Flying Squirrel* and *The Caboose Who Got Loose,* his success is all the more resounding for the chance that he takes.

What this book contains, then, is not really a set of "rules" at all, but one editor's appraisal of what constitutes a picture book, with the norms and conventions of the form as they have developed. Writing as a working editor, I am talking from a position of strength, because such

A very old woman who wants a cat is confronted with a mind-boggling array of Millions of Cats *in Wanda Gág's landmark picture book.*

an overwhelming majority of the successful picture books illustrate the points I believe are worth making. But I am only one editor, and there are doubtless dozens of others who will disagree with much of what I say. Time-honored as the use of animal characters is, for instance, for reasons I have explored in these pages, there are editors who find the idea of a talking animal abhorrent. Unrelenting didacticism is a bore, but Munro Leaf's old standbys *Manners Can Be Fun* and *Safety Can Be Fun* tickle me as much as an adult as they did when I was a child.

At least one thing I stress meets with universal agreement among editors: the importance of understanding the art and production aspects of publishing children's picture books. The pictures in this book are as important as the words. I have tried to include examples that are truly worth the proverbial thousand words, pictures that speak volumes about the illustrator's contribution to your writing. *Study them, and study the books cited in the bibliography.*

The illustration field has conventions—and economic considerations—that seem every bit as confining as writing norms and conventions; and again, there are ways around them. When you learn that your book is to be illustrated in black and white instead of the glorious technicolor you envisioned, remember that *In The Forest* and *Millions of Cats,* two of the greatest (and most successful) picture books ever written, are printed in black and white only. It is always possible to substitute another color for the black, as Robert McCloskey did in *Blueberries for Sal.* And take a look at *Andy and the Lion* to see how far the use of just one extra color, used imaginatively, will go to enliven the page.

There are myriad variations on the production theme, and the more you know about the limitations—and possibilities—the stronger the position you will be in to exploit them in *your* book. Bear in mind, though, that any good editor will rightly resist pure gimmickry, devices and tricks used for their own sake. Unless you are sure the idea you come up with is truly an integral part of the book, think again. John Goodall, the creator of *The Ballooning Adventures of Paddy Pork* and *Shrewbetinna's Birthday,* alternates half-page illustrations—the page actually half the size of the format—with whole pages, each page turn providing a new twist in the plot and a larger look at his entrancing land-scapes and interiors. No need for words; these are books the child can truly "read" for himself. Peter Newell wrote a story called *The Hole Book* about a bullet that travels through a landscape full of hilarious sur-prises until it lands in a wedding cake—and the book is pierced with an actual hole from front to back. *Tony's Tunnel,* Ann Sperry McGrath's engaging story about a small boy's secret hiding place, has a die cut throughout, defining the tunnel in a physical dimension. And remem-ber *Pat the Bunny,* with the fluffy cotton tail available on one page for the child to rub? Understanding what is possible expands opportunities for imagination and originality in your book.

If you follow the advice in these pages as though it were a no-fail recipe, you are probably going to be disappointed with the results. The essential ingredient—the one no writing manual can provide—won't be found in the pages of this book; you must find it in yourself. Inspira-tion, and then discipline, come from inside.

Writers draw inspiration from diverse and surprising sources; and probably Tom Edison was right when he described genius as "one percent inspiration and ninety-nine percent perspiration." Daniel Manus Pinkwater, the author of such picture books as *Bear's Picture* and *Around Fred's Bed,* has this to say on work and inspiration:

> My method and theory of art: I have this desk. When I spend a number of hours per day seated at it, I usually end up having written or drawn something. When I don't sit, I don't write or draw because when the writing or drawing comes around, I am fooling with the dogs, talking on the phone, or fixing the stairs. My artistic production is of higher quality than my imagination, skill, or intelligence would suggest, which leads me to believe that those faculties have very little to do with it. I would not take a million dollars for that desk.

So as you sit at *your* desk—or kitchen table, or favorite chair, or whatever work space you have jealously made your own—have this book with you for guidance to get you started. That's what it is meant to do. But look inside yourself for ideas and dreams that will become books children will love.

A GLOSSARY OF PRODUCTION TERMS

a.a. Author's alteration. A change in the galleys, made by the author, which is *not* part of the manuscript that author and editor have previously approved to send out for typesetting. The author bears the expense of author's alterations over and above a percentage stated in the contract.

acetate A treated sheet of plastic which is placed on top of the artist's line drawing to indicate where a color lies. An acetate overlay for each of the primary colors and black is placed to lie over the line drawing.

binder's boards Heavyweight cardboard around which the cover is wrapped to form the book's *case*.

binding die An engraving in metal or plastic which is used to stamp the book's case with the author's name, title of the book, standard book number, and publisher's name.

bleed An illustration that extends to the very edge of the page, with no margins.

blues (short for **blue-line prints**) A photocopy of the film from which the printer will make the final plates for printing, printed in blue.

bulk The thickness of the finished book, which varies according to the paper used. Publishers sometimes choose a porous paper with inferior printing quality in order to "bulk up" a picture book, i.e., make it look thicker than it would printed on a better-quality coated paper.

camera copy *Mechanicals* of the text placed in position, and the artwork either placed or indicated in position. The printer photographs the camera copy to make the films from which he prints the book.

camera-separated artwork Artwork photographed through a series of filters to separate each of the three primary colors and black. The colors must be separated for printing, as a different printing plate is used for each color.

case The cover of a book inside which the binder's boards are placed and glued.

castoff An estimate of how long the book will be. Designers cast off the type for picture books to show editors how much of the page must be devoted to type.

chromalins When artwork is separated by camera, the proofs for each color are printed separately, then together, on pieces of clear acetate specially treated to give an idea of how the color registers. Also known as dye transfer prints.

double-page spread or **spread** Two facing pages which may share a single illustration.

dummy A preliminary layout of the entire book. Designers prepare a dummy to show type layout, editors prepare a dummy to show pacing of the story, artists prepare a dummy to indicate, usually very roughly, where illustrations are to fall and what elements the illustrations will contain.

endpapers Heavy protective paper glued inside the case to absorb excess glue and hide the sewing of the binding.

F&Gs Folded and gathered sheets. (The British call them F&Cs for folded and collated sheets.) The F&Gs are the final printed sheets, which have been folded, gathered, and cut into pages following the proper sequence.

flat The final films of the text and the illustrations, taped into place on large sheets of heavy yellow paper (called goldenrods), which are used in platemaking.

flat sheet The sheet, usually about three feet by six feet, as it comes off the press.

fountain or **font** Wells of ink which can be adjusted to distribute ink to the printing press rollers.

four-color printing Using either hand-separated art or camera-separated art, the book is printed in four colors, usually the three primary colors and black, to achieve a full spectrum of color. Four-color printing is usually done on a four-color press, but sometimes it is printed on a two-color press by being run through the press two separate times.

galley proofs Long, narrow sheets on which the text is printed. Galley proofs usually are ordered before final reproduction proofs in order to make small corrections.

galley reproduction proofs The final proofs, used for camera copy, of text set into type. The repro proofs, as they are usually called, are printed on hard coated stock for sharp contrast between the black of the letters and the white spaces surrounding them.

goldenrod A dark yellow paper, specially treated to be opaque, on which the final films are positioned to make the plates.

halftone A continuous tone, like a photograph, including all shades of a color from its palest to a solid color.

key plate The base plate used in printing. It is usually the black plate, and its outlines guide the application of color in the printing.

layout A working diagram of a page, with type, illustrations, and margins indicated in correct position.

line art The basic cartoon illustration you see in the daily comics. Only the solid line is in black (or another color); the rest of the art area is stark white.

margin The area of the page that is left blank. The four margins are: front (the right-hand side of the page); gutter (the inner side of the page); head (the top of the page); and bottom.

mechanical A piece of heavy paper or board on which the art and text have been pasted, in their final form, to be shot by the printer's camera to make films.

offset The universally used printing process for color illustrations in children's books, in which the press offsets the image onto the paper from the plates using two ink-coated cylinders.

opaquing A costly hand process of painting the areas of a color-plate film which are *not* to be covered in that color.

p.e. Printer's error. A holdover from the days when printers were typesetters as well, a printer's error is a mistake make by the compositor in setting the manuscript into type. The typesetter absorbs the costs of printer's errors.

photostat A photocopy of the original artwork which gives an exact-size reproduction of the artwork. (Most office photocopiers distort size somewhat.)

plant costs or **origination costs** The first (and most often only) costs of preparing a book which do not vary as the costs of paper, ink, and binding materials do. It is the plant costs of color separation that make picture books so expensive to publish.

progressive proofs or **progs** Usually made of four-color artwork and practically always made for camera-separated artwork. They show each color alone, each color in combination with each of the other colors, and finally, the four colors together. They are indispensable to the artist and art director, who use them to guide the printer in making adjustments in the application of colors once the job is on press. Progs are supplied by the color separator.

proofs Approval copies of either the text set into type (see galley proofs) or color separations printed on a single page. The proof stage of any typesetting or printing job is the last point at which changes can be made without prohibitive expense.

register The perfect alignment of the color plates in a multicolor printing job.

sewing The way in which the signatures are bound into the case. There are three kinds of sewing in the binding of children's books: smyth sewing, which stitches the signatures together and is locked at the back; saddle sewing, which stitches around the signatures; and side sewing, in which the signatures are stitched to one another and the case.

signature An eight-, sixteen-, or thirty-two-page group of pages which results from the press sheet being folded and cut. Most picture books are printed in two sixteen-page signatures.

specifications or **specs** The manufacturing instructions for the book, indicating what kind of paper, what ink colors, what weight of binders board, and what kind of sewing will be used to produce the book.

trim size The final size of the page (not the case!) once the press sheet has been cut and folded into signatures.

BIBLIOGRAPHY

Children's Picture Books

Albert's Toothache. Barbara Williams. Dutton, 1974. A communications problem in a family of turtles.

All About Mud. Oliver Selfridge and Jerry Joyner. Addison-Wesley, 1978. As the title promises, with charming illustrations.

Always Room for One More. Sorche Nic Leodhas. Holt, Rinehart & Winston, 1965. A traditional tale, retold with Caldecott-caliber illustrations.

And to Think That I Saw It on Mulberry Street. Dr. Seuss. Vanguard, 1939. The protagonist devises a tall tale and decides to keep it to himself.

Andy and the Lion. James Daugherty. Viking, 1938. A small-town boy befriends a lion in this spoof of the Androcles story.

Andy: That's My Name. Tomie de Paola. Prentice-Hall, 1973. The youngest kid on the block shares his toys in this phonetic panorama.

Angus and the Ducks. Marjorie Flack. Doubleday, 1943. Angus lets his curiosity get the best of him, but only briefly.

Around Fred's Bed. Daniel Manus Pinkwater. Prentice-Hall, 1976. A lizard monster has trouble sleeping in this twisted bedtime tale.

The Art and Industry of Sandcastles. Jan Adkins. Walker, 1971. Profusely illustrated and carefully delineated, this is an unusual how-to.

Ballpoint Bananas. Charles Keller. Prentice-Hall, 1973. A long collection of bad jokes for the very young, profusely illustrated.

A Bargain for Frances. Russell Hoban. Harper & Row, 1970. Frances the badger beats her pal Thelma at her own game.

The Beast of Monsieur Racine. Tomi Ungerer. Farrar, Straus, & Giroux, 1971. A mysterious monster complicates a gentleman's life until it reveals itself as two children and an old blanket.

Behind the Wheel. Edward Koren. Holt, Rinehart & Winston, 1973. Odd beasts man the controls of a variety of mechanistic marvels.

Benjamin and Tulip. Rosemary Wells. Dial, 1973. Gentle but inspired warfare between two friends.

Benjamin's 365 Birthdays. Judi and Ron Barrett. Atheneum, 1974. Benjamin gets wrapped up in presents in this hilarious birthday saga.

Best Friends for Frances. Russell Hoban. Harper & Row, 1969. Frances and her sister ally themselves with a third friend in this roundabout but realistic story.

Billions of Bugs. Haris Petie. Prentice-Hall, 1975. Counting by 100s to a thousand, the author groups insects on the page according to their natural habits.

A Birthday for Frances. Russell Hoban. Harper & Row, 1968. Gloria's birthday brings out sibling jealousy in Frances, but her parents help her through it—just barely, as in real life.

Blueberries for Sal. Robert McCloskey. Viking, 1948. Parallel stories of a little girl and her mother and a bear and her cub on a mountain in Maine.

Boo! Bernard Most. Prentice-Hall, 1979. A frightened little monster overcomes his fear of people, with practice.

The Box with Red Wheels. Maud and Miska Petersham. Macmillan, 1949. A baby's encounter with barnyard animals, and vice versa.

The Caboose Who Got Loose. Bill Peet. Houghton Mifflin, 1964. A caboose finds a home in the trees.

Caesar, Cock of the Village. Philippe Dumas. Prentice-Hall, 1979. A weather cock comes down from his perch to discover the realities of small-town life for a real rooster.

Caps for Sale. Esphyr Slobodkina. Addison-Wesley, 1947. A peddler loses his caps to a troop of monkeys and recovers them by happy accident.

The Cat and the Collector. Linda Glovach. Prentice-Hall, 1972. An old man quarrels with his cat after the cat kills his other pet, a bird.

Chanticleer and the Fox. Barbara Cooney. Crowell, 1958. An adaptation of the Nun's Priest's Tale from the *Canterbury Tales,* this is the struggle between a fox and a rooster.

Charlie Needs a Cloak. Tomie de Paola. Prentice-Hall, 1974. A shepherd makes a new wool cloak, with no thanks to his pet sheep.

Clever Bill. William Nicholson. Farrar, Straus & Giroux, 1977. A reissue of the 1920s classic.

Colors. John Reiss. Bradbury, 1969. A systematic and stunning introduction to color.

Corduroy. Don Freeman. Viking, 1968. Corduroy searches for a lost button while a little girl searches for a way to buy him for her own.

Crow Boy. Taro Yashima. Viking, 1955. A shy country boy finds a place for himself with the help of an understanding teacher.

Curious George. H.A. Rey. Houghton Mifflin, 1941. A naughty little monkey is "rescued" from the jungle and causes trouble when he arrives in America.

Daffynitions. Charles Keller. Prentice-Hall, 1976. A collection of pun-filled, fun-filled definitions for common words.

Danny and His Thumb. Kathryn F. Ernst. Prentice-Hall, 1973. A little boy beats his thumb-sucking problem in a reassuring story.

David and Dog. Shirley Hughes. Prentice-Hall, 1978. A big sister helps out when David loses his stuffed dog.

Dinosaur Do's and Don'ts. Syd Hoff. Windmill, 1973. Short text and funny pictures show dinosaurs behaving and misbehaving.

Dinosaur Do's and Don'ts. Jean Burt Polhamus. Prentice-Hall, 1973. Rhymes with a humorous tone exhort children to behave with dinosaur examples.

Dorrie and the Amazing Elixir. 1974
Dorrie and the Birthday Eggs. 1971
Dorrie and the Blue Witch. 1964
Dorrie and the Fortune Teller. 1973
Dorrie and the Goblin. 1972
Dorrie and the Halloween Plot. 1976
Dorrie and the Haunted House. 1976
Dorrie and the Screenbit Ghost. 1979
Dorrie and the Weather Box. 1966
Patricia Coombs. Lothrop, Lee & Shepard. Adventures of a little witch named Dorrie in the worlds of sorcery and witchcraft.

Dracula's Cat. Jan Wahl. Prentice-Hall, 1978. A pet's-eye view of the monster.

Drummer Hoff. Ed and Barbara Emberley. Prentice-Hall, 1967. A cumulative text ends in a surprising way in this colorful picture book.

The Erie Canal. Peter Spier. Doubleday, 1970. The favorite song is expanded with busy pictures.

The Five Chinese Brothers. Claire Huchet Bishop. Coward, 1938. Superhuman feats of his brothers save a Chinese boy's life.

The Fleas of the Panther. Mariana Prieto. Prentice-Hall, 1975. A Spanish/English joke book within the reach of beginning readers.

Fortunately. Remy Charlip. Four Winds, 1964. By contrasting "fortunately" with "unfortunately," our hero undergoes a series of adventures culminating in a birthday party.

Fourteen Rats and a Rat Catcher. James Cressey. Prentice-Hall, 1977. Two points of view persist in this telling of an old lady's struggle with the rats who haunt her house.

Fox Went Out on a Chilly Night. Peter Spier. Doubleday, 1967. A folk song admirably adapted to a picture book adventure.

Frankenstein's Dog. Jan Wahl. Prentice-Hall, 1977. Another pet's-eye view, this time showing a pup's impatience with the monster's awkward ways.

Frederick. Leo Lionni. Pantheon, 1966. A field mouse saves up words and colors to share with his family over the long winter.

George and Martha. James Marshall. Houghton Mifflin, 1972. A pair of hippos enjoy the trials and tribulations of friendship in a set of stories.

George the Babysitter. Shirley Hughes. Prentice-Hall, 1978. When Mother goes to work, long-haired George babysits for three children. Hilarious.

Goldie the Dollmaker. M.B. Goffstein. Farrar, Straus & Giroux, 1980. The seemingly effortless drawings and story show the effort needed for perfection.

Handmade Secret Hiding Places. Nonny Hogrogian. Overlook Press, 1975. An array of places children can build themselves for games and make-believe.

Hansel and Gretel. Illustrated by Adrienne Adams; translated by Charles Scribner, Jr. Scribner, 1976. A retelling with highly symbolic illustrations that are easy to follow and offer food for thought.

Harry: A True Story. Blanche Dorsky. Prentice-Hall, 1977. A nursery school class's true account of what happened when their pet rabbit Harry became pregnant.

Harry the Dirty Dog. Gene Zion. Harper & Row, 1956. A dog who escapes his bath almost escapes recognition by his family.

I Wish I Was Sick Too. Franz Brandenberg. Greenwillow, 1976. The joys and tensions of being sick recaptured with charming pictures.

In the Forest. Marie Hall Ets. Viking, 1944. A little boy's odyssey with the animals in the forest.

In the Night Kitchen. Maurice Sendak. Harper & Row, 1970. Mickey discovers the joys of staying up late as he helps the bakers in this comic book-inspired fantasy.

Johnny Mapleleaf. Alvin Tresselt. Lothrop, Lee & Shepard, 1948. The life history of a leaf which explains life and death matter-of-factly.

Katy and the Big Snow. Virginia Lee Burton. Houghton Mifflin, 1943. A tractor has her turn to shine in this story of a winter storm.

Lito the Shoeshine Boy. David Mangurian. Four Winds, 1975. A photo documentary of a young boy in Central America making his way.

Little Black Sambo. Helen Bannerman. Platt and Munk, 1977. A reissue of the favorite story of the little boy who recovers his clothes from the tigers and has a fine meal of pancakes as a finale.

The Little Engine That Could. Watty Piper. Platt and Munk, 1976. Another reissue with new illustrations, this telling how the train loaded with good things for children gets over the mountain.

Little Toot. Hardie Gramatky. Putnam, 1939. A tugboat, too small to be of much account, saves the day when disaster strikes at sea.

Lobo and Brewster. Gladys Y. Cretan. Lothrop, Lee & Shepard, 1971. A nicely disguised story of sibling rivalry as a dog and cat make peace.

London Bridge Is Falling Down. Peter Spier. Doubleday, 1967. Yet another song profusely illustrated by the master artist.

Lumberjack. William Kurelek. Houghton Mifflin, 1974. Reminiscences of Canadian boyhood by a talented writer and painter.

Lyle, Lyle, Crocodile. 1965
Lyle and the Birthday Party. 1966
Lovable Lyle. 1969
Bernard Waber. Houghton Mifflin. The adventures of a crocodile who finds a home in New York City with the Primm family.

Madeline. 1939
Madeline and the Bad Hat. 1962
Madeline and the Gypsies. 1957
Madeline's Rescue. 1962
Ludwig Bemelmans. Viking. The adventures of the smallest girl in a French convent school.

Make Way for Ducklings. Robert McCloskey. Viking, 1941. Mr. and Mrs. Mallard look for a proper place to raise their family.

Masquerade. Kit Williams. Schocken, 1980. A fable containing hidden clues to the whereabouts of a gold treasure.

May I Stay? Harry Allard. Prentice-Hall, 1978. An adaptation of a ninth-century Norse legend wherein a traveler seeks a place to spend the night.

Mei Li. Thomas Handforth. Doubleday, 1938. The best part of running off to the fair is coming home again.

Merle, the High Flying Squirrel. Bill Peet. Houghton Mifflin, 1974. A squirrel with a special talent finds a place in the woods.

Merry Ever After. Joe Lasker. Viking, 1976. Two couples, one high-born, the other peasants, find happiness in medieval wedding celebrations.

Millions of Cats. Wanda Gág. Coward, McCann, 1928. A very old woman finds one cat after her husband brings home millions and billions of cats.

Minn of the Mississippi. Holling C. Holling. Houghton Mifflin, 1951. A turtle's life on the Mississippi River packed with loving detail in both text and pictures.

Miranda's Pilgrims. Rosemary Wells. Bradbury, 1969. Miranda's sleep is invaded by hard-working Pilgrims.

The Monster Riddle Book. Jane Sarnoff and Reynold Ruffins. Scribner, 1972. Profusely illustrated, this is a good collection of riddles on a monster theme for the youngest reader.

Moon Man. Tomi Ungerer. Harper & Row, 1967. The man in the moon participates in earthly activities before he returns to his moon again.

Mouse Café. Patricia Coombs. Lothrop, Lee & Shepard, 1972. A dazzling takeoff on the Cinderella story.

Mousekin's ABC. 1972
Mousekin's Close Call. 1978
Mousekin's Christmas Eve. 1965
Mousekin's Family. 1968
Mousekin Finds a Friend. 1967
Mousekin's Golden House. 1964
Mousekin Takes a Trip. 1976
Mousekin's Woodland Birthday. 1975
Mousekin's Woodland Sleepers. 1968
Edna Miller. Prentice-Hall. Realistic adventures of a white-footed mouse in the woods.

My Dentist. Harlow Rockwell. Greenwillow, 1975. A colorful and reassuring guide to what to expect from the dentist.

My Little Hen. Alice and Martin Provensen. Random House, 1973. A chicken is born in this simple but richly illustrated story.

My Visit to the Dinosaurs. Aliki. Crowell, 1969. A visit to the Museum of Natural History in New York City, with its stunning array of dinosaurs.

Nailheads and Potato Eyes. Cynthia Basil. Morrow, 1976. An introduction to metaphorical uses of words.

Nana Upstairs and Nana Downstairs. Tomie de Paola. Putnam, 1973. A little boy's view of his aging grandmother and her mother, dealing affectionately with the infirmities of old age.

Number 24. Guy Billout. Harlin Quist, 1973. A man waiting for a bus is witness to some amazing events.

One Morning in Maine. Robert McCloskey. Viking, 1952. Sally loses her first tooth in the midst of other events.

One Step...Two. Charlotte Zolotow. Lothrop, Lee & Shepard, 1981. A little girl takes her mother for a walk.

Outside Over There. Maurice Sendak. Harper & Row, 1981. A little girl rescues her baby sister from the goblins.

The Park Book. Charlotte Zolotow. Harper & Row, 1944. A day in the life of a city park, with its characteristic sights and sounds.

Pelle's New Suit. Elsa Beskow. Harper & Row, 1929. Pelle exchanges chores for the work that is required to make his new suit from wool to finished product.

Petunia. Roger Duvoisin. Knopf, 1950. Petunia is a silly goose who almost gets everyone in trouble believing she is wise because she carries a book under her arm.

Pierre. Maurice Sendak. Harper & Row, 1962. A cautionary tale about a little boy who professes not to care, written in rhyme.

Pleasant Fieldmouse. Jan Wahl. Harper & Row, 1964. An amiable fieldmouse enjoys some low-key adventures.

A Pocket for Corduroy. Don Freeman. Viking, 1978. Lisa loses her teddy bear as he searches for a pocket.

Push Pull, Empty Full: A Book of Opposites. Tana Hoban. Macmillan, 1972. A photographic exploration that contrasts opposite concepts.

Rain Drop Splash. Alvin Tresselt. Lothrop, Lee & Shepard, 1946. A poetic exploration of rain from the first drop on.

Rain Makes Applesauce. Julian Scheer. Holiday House, 1968. A nonsense compilation, economically told and extravagantly illustrated.

The Red Fire Book. James Trivers and J. Millman. Prentice-Hall, 1972. A story about a boy who follows fire safety rules to save his house.

Roar and More. Karla Kuskin. Harper & Row, 1956. Animal noises are graphically depicted in this simple but beautifully planned book.

Rotten Ralph. Jack Gantos. Houghton Mifflin, 1976. Ralph is a cat, and trouble is his medium, until he reforms.

The Runaway Bunny. Margaret Wise Brown. Harper & Row, 1972. A little bunny finds his plans to escape from his mother are thwarted in this charming, conversational book.

Sam, Bangs and Moonshine. Evaline Ness. Holt, Rinhart & Winston, 1966. Sam is a little girl full of "moonshine" and only when her lies cause trouble does she realize that she's hurting others.

See and Say. Antonio Frasconi. Harcourt Brace Jovanovich, 1955. Four languages are employed to identify common and uncommon objects depicted in colorful woodcuts.

The Seed the Squirrel Dropped. Haris Petie. Prentice-Hall, 1976. The life cycle of a tree is followed from seed to tree to fruit in this takeoff on "This Is the House That Jack Built."

The Sign on Rosie's Door. Maurice Sendak. Harper & Row, 1960. The antics of a bunch of kids in the city in summer, starring Rosie, an inventive dreamer.

The Snowy Day. Ezra Jack Keats. Viking, 1962. Peter discovers the joys of snow in this colorful book especially appealing to very young children.

Some Swell Pup. Maurice Sendak and Matthew Margolis. Farrar, Straus & Giroux, 1976. A guide to caring for dogs, done in comic strip form, containing all kinds of useful information.

Song of the Swallows. Leo Politi. Scribner, 1949. A boy makes friends with a man in this story set in the mission of San Juan Capistrano.

Stone Soup. Marcia Brown. Scribner, 1947. Set in France, this earthy folk tale shows how some hungry soldiers fool the selfish townspeople.

The Story of Babar. Jean de Brunhoff. Random House, 1937. An orphaned elephant finds his way in Paris with the help of a rich old lady.

Story About Ping. Marjorie Flack. Viking, 1933. A little duck on the Yangtze River searches for his family.

Strewwelpeter. Heinrich Hoffman. Routledge and Kegan Paul, 1909. Grisly cautionary tales about common childhood misbehavior.

The Stupids Have a Ball. 1978
The Stupids Die. 1981
The Stupids Step Out. 1977
Harry Allard. Houghton Mifflin. A family of charming idiots do everything wrong in this comic series.

Someone Small. Barbara Borack. Harper & Row, 1969. A little girl adjusts to the arrival of a baby sister as her parakeet grows and finally dies.

Sylvester and the Magic Pebble. William Steig. Farrar, Straus & Giroux, 1969. A donkey finds a magic pebble and gets into trouble until his parents inadvertently save him.

The Tale of Benjamin Bunny. Beatrix Potter. Warne, 1904. Benjamin and his more famous cousin Peter encounter a cat in Mr. McGregor's garden.

The Tale of the Flopsy Bunnies. Beatrix Potter. Warne, 1905. A mouse tries to save the six bunnies Mr. McGregor has put in a sack.

The Tale of Peter Rabbit. Beatrix Potter. Warne, 1902. Peter doesn't heed his mother's warnings and nearly gets caught in Mr. McGregor's garden.

The Tenth Good Thing About Barney. Judith Viorst. Atheneum, 1971. When Barney the cat dies, the tenth good thing reveals itself in this story of the cycle of life and death.

The Thanksgiving Story. Alice Dalgliesh. Scribner, 1954. A factual account with collage illustrations by Helen Sewall.

Three Little Pigs. Paul Galdone. Clarion, 1970. A spirited retelling of the favorite story, illustrated with verve.

Thy Friend, Obadiah. Brinton Turkle. Viking, 1969. A Quaker boy comes to terms with the seagull who follows him.

The Tiger Skin Rug. Gerald Rose. Prentice-Hall, 1978. A skinny tiger takes refuge in a house as a rug, but as he gets fatter and sleeker, he's in danger of being found out.

Too Funny for Words. Charles Keller. Prentice-Hall, 1973. A photographic joke book for young children, featuring gesture jokes.

Turn Over. Bernard Most. Prentice-Hall, 1979. A question is asked on one page and the answer presented when the reader "turns over" the page in this funny and inventive book.

The Velveteen Rabbit. Margery Williams. Doubleday, 1958. The velveteen rabbit discovers what it is to be real in this fantasy about a castoff toy.

What's in the Woods? June Goldsborough. Prentice-Hall, 1976. An alphabetical mystery story as the animals wonder what kind of animal the child visitor can be.

What to Do When There's No One But You. Harriet Gore. Prentice-Hall, 1974. A guide for very young children about medical emergencies, and what to do until adult help arrives.

Where the Wild Things Are. Maurice Sendak. Harper & Row, 1963. Max, sent to bed without supper for acting like a wild thing, imagines a trip to the island where the wild things are.

Whose Mouse Are You? Robert Kraus. Windmill, 1970. A lonely little mouse learns to give and take in this question-and-answer text.

Why Mosquitoes Buzz in People's Ears. Verna Aardema. Dial, 1975. An African folktale about the mosquito and why he suffers punishment.

Yummers! James Marshall. Houghton Mifflin, 1973. Emily Pig tries to go on a diet.

Audience

Butler, Dorothy. *Cushla and Her Books.* Horn Book, 1980.

Coody, Betty. *Using Literature with Young Children.* 2nd ed. William C. Brown, 1979.

Duke, Judith S. *Children's Books and Magazines: A Market Study.* Knowledge Industry Publications, 1979.

Gibson, Eleanor, and Levin, Harry. *The Psychology of Reading.* Cambridge: MIT Press, 1975.

Meek, Margaret, et al. *The Cool Web: The Pattern of Children's Reading.* Atheneum, 1978.

White, Dorothy. *Books Before Five.* Faber, 1963.

The Context of Children's Literature

Cameron, Eleanor. *The Green and Burning Tree: On the Writing and Enjoyment of Children's Books.* Little, Brown, 1969.

Egoff, Sheila, et al. ed. *Only Connect: Readings on Children's Literature.* University of Chicago Press, 1976.

Georgiou, Constantine. *Children and Their Literature.* Prentice-Hall, 1969.

Huck, Charlotte. *Children's Literature in the Elementary School.* Holt, Rinehart & Winston, 1979.

Larrick, Nancy. *A Teacher's Guide to Children's Books.* Charles E. Merrill, 1960.

Rollock, Barbara. *Black Experience in Children's Books,* New York: New York Public Library, 1974.

Sutherland, Zena, ed. *The Best in Children's Books, 1966-1972.* University of Chicago Press, 1973.

———————————— *The Best in Children's Books, 1973-1978.* University of Chicago Press, 1979.

———————————— and Arbuthnot, May Hill. *Children and Books,* 5th ed. Scott, Foresman, 1977.

On Writing and Publishing

Applebee, Arthur. *The Child's Concept of Story: Ages Two to Seventeen.* University of Chicago Press, 1981.

Bader, Barbara. *American Picture Books: From Noah's Ark to the Beast Within.* New York: Macmillan, 1976.

Bettelheim, Bruno. *The Uses of Enchantment,* Knopf, 1978.

Commire, Anne. *Something About the Author: Facts and Pictures about Contemporary Authors and Illustrators of Books for Young People.* Gale Research Company, 1975.

Greenfeld, Howard. *From Writer to Reader,* Crown. 1976.

Karl, Jean. *From Childhood to Childhood: Children's Books and Their Creators.* John Day, 1975.

Lanes, Selma. *Down the Rabbit Hole: Adventures and Misadventures in the Realm of Children's Literature.* Atheneum, 1976.

Lewis, Claudia. *Writing for Young Children.* Doubleday, 1981.

Wintle, Justin, and Fisher, Emma. *The Pied Pipers.* The Two Continents Publishing Group, 1974.

Wyndham, Lee. *Writing for Children and Teenagers.* Writer's Digest, 1968; revised edition, 1980.

Yolen, Jane. *Writing Books for Children.* The Writer, 1976.

INDEX

PERMISSION ACKNOWLEDGMENTS

ABOUT THE AUTHOR

Ellen Roberts has edited and published more than 500 books for children of all ages. She has been an editor with St. Martin's Press, Lothrop, Lee & Shepard, and Prentice-Hall. Among the more than 150 picture books she has published are winners of the Caldecott Medal, the Kate Greenaway Medal, and the Prix Graphique. She has discovered such talents as Charles Keller, Jean Polhamus, Dennis Nolan, Harry Allard, and Linda Glovach, and has guided these writers to careers as children's picture book authors. Roberts is a popular speaker, lecturing to writers' groups and classes at schools and universities throughout the country. This book combines observations and insights from her long experience behind the editor's desk with advice from many other children's picture book creators. Roberts is also the author of *Nonfiction for Children* and is the book review editor for *youngperson*.

Other Books of Interest

General Writing Books

Beginning Writer's Answer Book, edited by Polking and Bloss $14.95

Getting the Words Right: How to Revise, Edit and Rewrite, by Theodore A. Rees Cheney $13.95

How to Become a Bestselling Author, by Stan Corwin $14.95

How to Get Started in Writing, by Peggy Teeters (paper) $8.95

How to Write a Book Proposal, by Michael Larsen $9.95

How to Write While You Sleep, by Elizabeth Ross $12.95

If I Can Write, You Can Write, by Charlie Shedd $12.95

International Writers' & Artists' Yearbook (paper) $12.95

Law & the Writer, edited by Polking & Meranus (paper) $10.95

Knowing Where to Look: The Ultimate Guide to Research, by Lois Horowitz $16.95

Make Every Word Count, by Gary Provost (paper) $7.95

Pinckert's Practical Grammar, by Robert C. Pinckert $12.95

Teach Yourself to Write, by Evelyn Stenbock (paper) $9.95

The 29 Most Common Writing Mistakes & How to Avoid Them, by Judy Delton $9.95

Writer's Block & How to Use It, by Victoria Nelson $12.95

Writer's Guide to Research, by Lois Horowitz $9.95

Writer's Market, edited by Becky Williams $21.95

Writer's Resource Guide, edited by Bernadine Clark $16.95

Writing for the Joy of It, by Leonard Knott $11.95

Writing From the Inside Out, by Charlotte Edwards (paper) $9.95

Magazine/News Writing

Basic Magazine Writing, by Barbara Kevles $16.95

How to Sell Every Magazine Article You Write, by Lisa Collier Cool $14.95

How to Write & Sell the 8 Easiest Article Types, by Helene Schellenberg Barnhart $14.95

Writing Nonfiction that Sells, by Samm Sinclair Baker $14.95

Fiction Writing

Creating Short Fiction, by Damon Knight (paper) $8.95

Fiction Writer's Help Book, by Maxine Rock $12.95

Fiction Writer's Market, edited by Jean Fredette $18.95

Handbook of Short Story Writing, by Dickson and Smythe (paper) $8.95

How to Write & Sell Your First Novel, by Oscar Collier with Frances Spatz Leighton $14.95

How to Write Short Stories that Sell, by Louise Boggess (paper) $7.95

One Way to Write Your Novel, by Dick Perry (paper) $6.95

Storycrafting, by Paul Darcy Boles $14.95

Writing Romance Fiction—For Love And Money, by Helene Schellenberg Barnhart $14.95

Writing the Novel: From Plot to Print, by Lawrence Block (paper) $8.95

Special Interest Writing Books

Complete Book of Scriptwriting, by J. Michael Straczynski $14.95

The Complete Guide to Writing Software User Manuals, by Brad M. McGehee (paper) $14.95

The Craft of Comedy Writing, by Sol Saks $14.95

The Craft of Lyric Writing, by Sheila Davis $18.95

Guide to Greeting Card Writing, edited by Larry Sandman (paper) $8.95

How to Make Money Writing About Fitness & Health, by Celia & Thomas Scully $16.95

How to Make Money Writing Fillers, by Connie Emerson (paper) $8.95

How to Write a Cookbook and Get It Published, by Sara Pitzer $15.95

How to Write a Play, by Raymond Hull $13.95

How to Write and Sell Your Personal Experiences, by Lois Duncan (paper) $9.95

How to Write and Sell (Your Sense of) Humor, by Gene Perret (paper) $9.95
How to Write "How-To" Books and Articles, by Raymond Hull (paper) $8.95
How to Write the Story of Your Life, by Frank P. Thomas $12.95
How You Can Make $50,000 a Year as a Nature Photojournalist, by Bill Thomas (paper) $17.95
Mystery Writer's Handbook, by The Mystery Writers of America (paper) $8.95
Nonfiction for Children: How to Write It, How to Sell It, by Ellen E.M. Roberts $16.95
On Being a Poet, by Judson Jerome $14.95
The Poet's Handbook, by Judson Jerome (paper) $8.95
Poet's Market, by Judson Jerome $16.95
Sell Copy, by Webster Kuswa $11.95
Successful Outdoor Writing, by Jack Samson $11.95
Travel Writer's Handbook, by Louise Zobel (paper) $9.95
TV Scriptwriter's Handbook, by Alfred Brenner (paper) $9.95
Writing After 50, by Leonard L. Knott $12.95
Writing and Selling Science Fiction, by Science Fiction Writers of America (paper) $7.95
Writing for Children & Teenagers, by Lee Wyndham (paper) $9.95
Writing for the Soaps, by Jean Rouverol $14.95
Writing the Modern Mystery, by Barbara Norville $15.95
Writing to Inspire, by Gentz, Roddy, et al $14.95

The Writing Business

Complete Guide to Self-Publishing, by Tom & Marilyn Ross $19.95
Complete Handbook for Freelance Writers, by Kay Cassill $14.95
Editing for Print, by Geoffrey Rogers $14.95
Freelance Jobs for Writers, edited by Kirk Polking (paper) $8.95
How to Bulletproof Your Manuscript, by Bruce Henderson $9.95
How to Get Your Book Published, by Herbert W. Bell $15.95
How to Understand and Negotiate a Book Contract or Magazine Agreement, by Richard Balkin $11.95
How You Can Make $20,000 a Year Writing, by Nancy Hanson (paper) $6.95
Literary Agents: How to Get & Work with the Right One for You, by Michael Larsen $9.95
Professional Etiquette for Writers, by William Brohaugh $9.95

To order directly from the publisher, include $2.00 postage and handling for 1 book and 50¢ for each additional book. Allow 30 days for delivery.

Writer's Digest Books, Department B
9933 Alliance Road, Cincinnati OH 45242
Prices subject to change without notice.